CW00386194

First published in 2019 by Fine Feather Press Limited
The Coach House, Elstead Road, Farnham, Surrey GU10 1JE

Copyright © 2019 Fine Feather Press Limited

All rights reserved. No part of this publication may be reproduced,
stored in a retrieval system or transmitted in any form or by any means,
electronic, mechanical, photocopying, recording or otherwise, without the
prior permission of the publishers.

2 4 6 8 10 9 7 5 3 1

A CIP catalogue record is available from the British Library

ISBN: 978-1-908489-40-1
Printed in China

FFP

Fine Feather Press

www.finefeatherpress.com

CONTENTS

General Colour

Note whether the bird has a particular colour or pattern, such as the blue tit's yellow chest or the magpie's black-and-white feathers. Soon, a mere glimpse of these basic colours will help you to identify a bird instantly.

Beak Shape

Birds belong to families that share similar features, such as beak shape. By recognising the family, you are close to being able to identify a particular bird.

 Strong finch beaks are good for cracking seeds.

 Hawks have hooked ones for tearing meat.

 Woodpeckers use their beaks for drilling holes and drumming on trees.

 Treecreepers have long, curved ones for picking out insects from bark.

 Tits have thin beaks for catching insects.

 Crow beaks allow them to eat almost anything.

HOW TO IDENTIFY BIRDS
OVERALL APPEARANCE

In order to see birds it is necessary to become a part of the silence.
Robert Lynd, writer (1879–1949)

THE WHEEL HELPS YOU to identify birds where you most need to – outside – and working alongside it is this book. Here lie some pointers for those new to the subject, along with profiles of the garden birds featured on the wheel. Reading about them can be fascinating – but nothing beats simply stopping and watching and listening to the bird world around you.

FIELD MARKINGS

Crown · Head · Cheek · Nape · Shoulder · Back · Wing · Tail · Rump · Side · Thigh · Leg · Upper beak · Lower beak · Throat · Breast · Belly

This diagram shows the parts of a bird often referred to in this guidebook, such as the goldcrest's yellow crown, the male woodpecker's red nape or the house martin's white rump. Look out for particular field markings such as these: they are clues that help you to determine a bird's identity.

Male or Female?

Female · Male

When trying to identify a bird, remember that not all male and female birds look alike. The colouring may vary completely, as with male and female pheasants, or may change only in certain places as with the chest feathers in these bullfinches.

Fledglings

Robin

Is the bird you are spotting young? If so, it may not look like its parents. This young robin fledgling was speckled and is just getting its red breast feathers.

WHAT SIZE AND WHERE IS IT?

It helps to compare the size of the bird you are watching to that of one you already know, as this will help to narrow down the options as to what that bird could be.

Think about the location you are seeing it in, too. A tiny bird in the undergrowth is likely to be a wren, while one high up in conifer trees might well be a goldcrest.

 Wren

 Dunnock

 Blackbird

 Green woodpecker

TAIL SHAPE

Tails help to steer, brake and impress the opposite sex. Some birds have distinctive tail shapes, making identification easier.

Pheasant

Jays, sparrowhawks, magpies, long-tailed tits, wagtails and pheasants all have long tails.

House martin

Swallows, swifts and house martins have notched tails but only the last has a white rump.

Waxwing

The tail of the waxwing is square in flight, as are those of the starling and thrush family.

UP IN THE AIR

JIZZ IS A STRANGE WORD that people use to describe the overall impression a bird makes. It may be based on its appearance, how it behaves as well as how it flies and is something you become better at sensing as you observe birds over time. In flight, jizz may be the shape a bird makes in the sky, the way it flies or some particular flight markings.

FLIGHT PATTERNS

Although not all birds can fly, the ones featured here can. Some, like the swift, seem to be made for flight – landing only to breed – while others, such as the pheasant, seem to struggle to lift their heavy bodies off the ground. Once airborne, birds make different patterns as they fly – some travel in straight lines, some swoop up and down, while others don't seem to follow any path at all.

Finches and sparrows have short wings and often bounding flight patterns.

Woodpeckers have very obvious undulating flight patterns.

Starlings, like waxwings and thrushes, fly in a direct line.

WING SHAPE

Look at the size and shape of a bird's wings, as well as the speed with which it beats them, to help you work out its identity.

Swift

Though the screaming sound of swifts is unmistakable, their long, curved wings are distinctive too.

Great tit

Tits have small, rounded wings (though not as tiny as the wren's) which beat rapidly in flight.

Jay

Many larger birds such as the jay have broad wings for flying fast or for soaring.

FLIGHT STYLES

Pigeon gliding

Small birds tend to flap continuously; larger ones save energy by gliding or soaring on air currents; and kestrels are famous for hovering.

Certain markings show up only in flight, like the yellow wing bars on this goldfinch.

Goldfinch flapping

Kestrel hovering

SPRING ARRIVALS

Many birds arrive in spring to breed, including swifts, house martins, spotted flycatchers, garden warblers and swallows. They winter in warmer places such as Africa, the Middle East and around the Mediterranean.

Spotted flycatcher

Swallow

Garden warbler

AUTUMN ARRIVALS

Birds that migrate here in the autumn come in search of food and to escape harsher weather conditions in their breeding grounds. The UK's resident bird population also rises at this time with visitors from abroad.

Redwing

Fieldfare

Brambling

Waxwing

BIRD BEHAVIOUR

THIS IS ONE OF THE FINAL PIECES in the bird-identification puzzle. Each species displays its own patterns of behaviour, which change with the seasons. If you look around you, wherever you live, there will be birds going about their daily business. Here are some things to keep an eye out for.

THE SOUND OF BIRDS

Learning bird song is one of the best gateways to bird identification, and knowing even a few makes walks outside fascinating. Most birds make an impressive array of sounds which they use for situations ranging from wooing to warning.

Robin

Long-tailed tits

BIRD SONGS

Song is used mainly in the spring as a way for males to attract a mate and to defend their territories. Most birds become quiet when breeding is over.

CONTACT CALLS

These are simpler than songs and are a way for one bird to pass information to another. Flocks use them to signal danger, their location or food.

Blue tit

ALARM CALLS

Many surprisingly small birds such as wrens and blue tits make very loud, harsh calls of alarm in the face of danger and will challenge intruders.

BEGGING CALLS

Listen out in the spring for the demanding cries of hungry chicks in their nests, trying to get their parents to put food into their open beaks.

Chiffchaff

FLIGHT CALLS

These are sounds made by birds during periods of flight, particularly when they are migrating – they may be made during the day or at night.

DAWN CHORUS

In temperate zones like the UK, spring marks the breeding season for birds. From just before sunrise, birds strike up in order, singing to attract a mate.

SUMMER MOULT

Moulting jackdaw

By the end of the breeding season, many birds look rather ragged and in August and early September they seem to disappear. This is when they are going through their annual moult – a time for shedding worn-out feathers and growing new ones. Some birds may moult twice or even three times a year.

WINTER FLOCKING

Once breeding is over and birds have finished moulting, some species such as long-tailed tits and goldfinches form flocks that forage for food by day and may roost together at night. In spring, these groups disband as individuals each look for a mate.

Starlings perform extraordinary displays in the autumn and winter: thousands of them swirl through in the sky in what are known as murmurations.

THE BIRDWATCHING YEAR

THERE IS A THRILL TO BE HAD seeing the first house martins arrive in the spring or watching starlings circling in their thousands in one of their murmurations. Listed below are some of the key events to look out for during the course of the year that mark the seasons and are a delight in themselves.

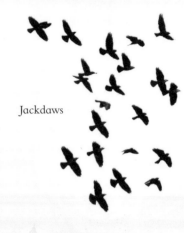

Jackdaws

Waxwing

Mistle thrush

Great tit

Great spotted woodpecker

Redpoll

Redwing

DECEMBER
Mistle thrushes can be heard singing from high perches even on wet days.

Fieldfares and redwings roam in flocks, gorging themselves on berries.

JANUARY
Early breeders such as blackbirds, song thrushes and great tits start singing.

Waxwings may be seen in flocks, stripping bushes of berries as they go.

FEBRUARY
Great spotted woodpeckers drum to defend territory and attract females.

The dawn and evening chorus build as daylight hours lengthen.

Bullfinch

Brambling

Blue tit

NOVEMBER
Listen out for tawny owls hooting from dusk to mark their territories.

Tit families band into larger groups, sometimes with nuthatches.

MARCH
Bullfinches, not often visible, descend to eat buds in hedgerows and on trees.

Bramblings, redpolls and siskins are on the move and may visit gardens.

Siskin

Tawny owl

OCTOBER
Fieldfares, redwings, waxwings and bramblings arrive for the winter.

Look for murmurations – vast flocks of starlings swirling in the sky.

House martin

Starlings

WINTER · SPRING · SUMMER · AUTUMN

APRIL
Look out for the arrival of house martins, blackcaps and garden warblers.

The dawn chorus is now in full swing and will be for the next two months.

Yellowhammer

Fieldfare

SEPTEMBER
House martins gather on wires, often near water, before flying south.

Charms of goldfinches forage for seeds in scrubby areas and fields.

MAY
The last swifts and spotted flycatchers arrive, marking the end of migration.

Most birds have built their nests by now and are busy feeding their chicks.

Swift

Goldfinch

AUGUST
Many birds now disappear from view during their annual moult.

Blackbirds may well be on to their third brood of the season.

JULY
Look out for fledglings often sporting different plumage to the adults.

Swifts start to leave this month, with most having left by mid-August.

JUNE
Bird song dwindles while the cries of young chicks hungry for food increase.

Thrushes and blackbirds continue to sing, especially in the evening.

Spotted flycatcher

Blackbird

Starling fledgling

Song thrush

Sparrow fledgling

BIRD FEEDERS

Birds feed in a variety of ways – thrushes and robins eat from the ground or tables, while great spotted woodpeckers, tits and finches cling to hanging feeders. Keeping food apart deters squabbling, and cleaning areas regularly will help to prevent diseases such as avian pox.

IN THE GARDEN
HOW TO ATTRACT BIRDS

Everyone likes birds. What wild creature is more accessible to our eyes and ears, as close to us and everyone in the world, as universal as a bird?
Sir David Attenborough, naturalist (born 1926)

ENCOURAGING BIRDS into your garden is easy – all you need to provide is water, suitable food and, if possible, nest sites. It can take a while for them to be discovered, so don't despair if your efforts seem to go unnoticed at first.

NEST BOXES

You can buy ready-made nest boxes suitable for specific species such as the blue-tit one below. These need to be fixed firmly in a sheltered place away from the reach of potential predators. You could try nailing old shoes to trees or leaving flower pots secreted in ivy or undergrowth.

UNWANTED VISITORS

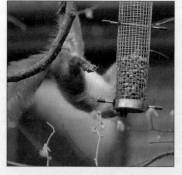

Not all animals dining at your feeders are equally welcome. Multiple food stations help to stop bully birds such as magpies dominating. Deterring acrobatic and determined squirrels can be hard, but putting round lids over the tops of your feeders and placing them away from jumping-off points should help.

WINTERTIME

Freezing temperatures are bad for all birds and especially small ones such as wrens, goldcrests and blue tits. Keeping food supplies topped up and focusing on suet-based ones provides a lifeline for them at this time. Clean and dry nest boxes also make perfect roosting sites where birds can huddle to keep warm.

PLANTS TO GROW

There are many plants you can grow with seeds and berries which birds love to eat. Thrushes gorge on holly, elder, rowan and hawthorn berries; finches and tits eat the seeds of thistles and sunflowers. Cheaper still is to allow a bed of weeds to flourish in the garden or just dig over the soil to let robins grab the worms.

SHALLOW BIRD BATHS

Birds need fresh water daily for drinking and bathing. Anything that mimics a shallow puddle is good, preferably with sloping edges or rocks sticking out from the surface. Birds bathe to rid themselves of dust and parasites and then preen their feathers to replace natural oils. Water is best changed daily in all seasons.

WHAT TO FEED THEM

BIRDS NEED DIFFERENT TYPES of food according to the season: fat-based ones during cold weather to help build their energy reserves and high-protein seeds when they are raising families. Here is a guide to what your commonest visitors like to eat.

HANGING FEEDERS

WOODPECKERS

Sharp great spotted woodpecker claws have no problem gripping wire feeders. These birds readily take peanuts and suet-seed mixes as long as they are hanging. Green woodpeckers scour grassy patches looking for ants instead.

FINCHES

All finches have sturdy beaks which make perfect seed-crackers. Pretty goldfinches are renowned for feasting messily on niger seeds and greenfinches on sunflowers, while finches will eat any type of seed you put out.

TITS

Tits feed at all angles from branches, so hanging feeders pose no difficulty for them. Peanuts are always popular but avoid these during the breeding season, as adults may feed them to chicks who may then choke.

SPARROWS

These are the hoovers of the bird world – always on the lookout for the odd scrap and hovering expectantly around cafés and picnic tables. They take leftovers on the ground or mixed seed from hanging feeding stations.

GROUND FEEDERS

THRUSHES

This family includes blackbirds and song and mistle thrushes. These ground feeders will take mealworm, sultanas and fruit scraps as well as the seed remains dropped by other birds on hanging feeders.

ROBINS

Canny robins watch gardeners digging, waiting for worms to be unearthed. Mealworms are an ideal food to leave out for them along with chopped fruit and grated hard cheese. Some robins will eat from your hand.

DUNNOCKS

Their habit of skulking along under bushes combined with their brown plumage makes dunnocks hard to spot. They may venture out to pick at fallen seeds from feeders or peck at grated cheese and breadcrumbs.

PIGEONS & DOVES

These birds always look monstrously large next to most common garden birds. They are almost exclusively seed feeders; the seed needs to be left on the ground or on a bird table to ensure that they can reach it.

BIRD FAMILIES

The birds that follow are grouped by families each of which, like yours, shares similar characteristics. This is a pair of male greenfinches – small songbirds found through most of Europe – with typical sturdy finch beaks, notched tails and rounded heads.

BIRD SPECIES

*A good ornithologist should be able to distinguish birds by
their air as well as by their colours and shape; on the ground
as well as on the wing, and in the bush as well as in the hand.*
Gilbert White, naturalist (1720–1793)

IDENTIFYING BIRDS often depends on having some
sort of guide to hand, which is what makes the
light and transportable birdspotting wheel so
useful. Once you have a name, this book will help
you to fill in the details, making identification
that much easier next time round.

Full profiles are given for the 44 species on the
wheel and there are some less common birds
featured at the end. This is not an exhaustive list
of garden birds, but is intended to make you less
exhausted when you're trying to find the one you
want, especially if you are new to birdwatching.

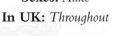

KEY FACTS

Found: *Gardens, parks, woods, hedgerows*
Length: *Up to 11.5 cm*
Present: *January to December*
Food: *Insects, seeds & fruit*
Often seen: *At a feeder*
Similar to: *Great tit*
Behaviour: *Bold*
Lives for: *Up to 10 years*
Nests: *In tree holes, nest boxes*
Eggs: *6 to 12 white speckled eggs, sometimes more*
Broods: *1 per year*
Sexes: *Alike*
In UK: *Throughout*

FLEDGLING

Baby blue tits are ready to leave the nest after 19 days. They will then stay with their parents for a few weeks, learning how to find food and avoid danger.

BLUE TIT
Cyanistes caeruleus

WHAT BETTER WAY TO START this guide than with the blue tit – one of our most common and cheery garden birds. It is both plentiful in number and easy to spot hopping among the branches of trees and bushes or acrobatically hanging from them searching for food. The male and female are alike, with pairs forming in the spring to breed before moulting and spending the colder months in flocks.

IN THE GARDEN

It is extremely rewarding when birds make their home in your garden and blue tits are very happy to live near humans. They will readily make use of any suitable nest boxes you put up and if you place a bird feeder in your garden, especially one containing peanuts, they will almost certainly be among the first to visit.

LOOK/LISTEN FOR

Blue cap and white face
•
Lemon-yellow belly
•
Thin black eye stripe and dark neck collar
•
Hanging acrobatically from branches while feeding
•
Very high-pitched song

VOICE

The blue tit's song starts off with two long high notes followed by a fast lower-pitched trill – roughly transcribed as "tsee-see-see-see". Other sounds include scolding alarm calls directed at any approaching threat and with head feathers raised; short contact calls to nearby birds as well as a range of noises made to its young.

NESTING

From March onwards, the female carries moss, grass, hair, wool and feathers to the nest site before she starts the egg-laying process. Eggs are laid at daily intervals until the clutch is complete, and the chicks hatch out 14 days later. Both parents then have the huge task of finding enough caterpillars to feed their hungry brood, with each chick eating around 10 of them a day. Some blue-tit parents look very ragged by the summer's end!

GREAT TIT
Parus major

LOOK/LISTEN FOR

Black breast stripe

•

Black cap and white cheeks

•

White wing bar

•

"Teacher–teacher" song
heard from late winter
onwards

•

Dominant behaviour
at bird feeders

VOICE

If you spend some time listening to these birds, you will discover that they are rarely quiet and have an incredibly wide range of songs and calls. The easiest one to recognise sounds a bit like "teacher–teacher" being repeatedly sung. Others include a shrill "tche-tche-tche" to warn away intruders and a classically bird-like "tweet-tweet-tweet" call.

THE TIT FAMILY

This is a large group of songbirds of which we have six in the UK – the great, blue, marsh, willow, coal and crested tits. All of them are small, active, noisy and agile birds which tend to form small flocks in the autumn and winter months. This means that there are more of them to look out for danger, find food and for keeping warm when roosting together at night.

KEY FACTS

Found: *Gardens, woods*
Length: *Up to 14 cm*
Present: *January to December*
Food: *Insects, seeds & fruit*
Often seen: *On a perch*
Similar to: *Blue tit*
Behaviour: *Sociable*
Lives for: *Up to 13 years*
Nests: *In holes in trees, rock crevices or nest boxes*
Eggs: *Up to 12 white speckled eggs*
Broods: *1 per year*
Sexes: *Female paler*
In UK: *Throughout*

THE INTENSITY OF THE YELLOW CHEST colour varies between individuals, with males having wider, longer stripes and yellower chests than the females. Juveniles look similar to the adults but have yellow rather than white cheeks. Research has shown that great tits have above average intelligence for their size and are able to memorise where other birds store food in order to steal it later on.

IN THE GARDEN

Great tits are a familiar sight at feeders – they are not fussy eaters and will take any type of seed as well as suet and mealworm. Unlike other members of the tit family, they occasionally feed on the ground. Nest boxes with wider openings than those for blue tits are used, as well as tree hollows or gaps in stone walls.

TOP "DOGS"

It doesn't take long to notice that great tits are top of the pecking order at feeding stations and will use their larger size to shoo away smaller blue or coal tits.

COAL TIT
Periparus ater

White mark on back of neck

•

Black bib and white cheeks

•

Pinkish underparts

•

Larger head than other tits

•

Dotted white lines on wings

•

Hopping about on the
branches of conifers

KEY FACTS

Found: *Gardens, woods*
Length: *11 cm*
Present: *January to December*
Food: *Small insects, spiders,
nuts, seeds & fruit*
Often seen: *On a perch*
Similar to: *Marsh tit*
Behaviour: *Nervous*
Lives for: *Up to 9 years*
Nests: *In tree holes, wall crevices*
Eggs: *7 to 9 white eggs with
red-brown speckles*
Broods: *1 to 2 per year*
Sexes: *Alike*
In UK: *Throughout*

ALTHOUGH NOT AS TINY as a wren or a goldcrest, the coal tit is still an appealingly small garden bird. Like the blue tit, it is constantly active and hangs at all angles from bird feeders and the outermost branches of tall conifer trees, reaching for food. Its small pointed beak is a useful tool for prising seeds out of cones – some of which may be hidden to eat later if not stolen by onlooking birds.

VOICE

The coal tit spends much of its time in the tops of conifer trees where it is hard to see or hear. Its song has the same high-pitched squeaky quality as that of the goldcrest, but it shifts between a higher and a lower note – a sort of "pee-chew, pee-chew, pee-chew" delivered at speed. When foraging in a group, it uses a variety of calls to stay in contact with the other birds and warn them of any danger.

COLOURING

The *ater* part of its scientific name means dusky black and relates to the dark back, head and chest patch as well as the black legs. The easiest way to identify a coal tit is by the white stripe on the back of its head which looks almost as though it has been mistakenly drawn on. Males and females are alike, though there is quite a range in both colour and size among coal tits across Europe.

NEST

The female lays her eggs in a soft, mossy nest, sometimes making use of old mouse holes or among tree roots. The young hatch after two weeks and fledge 16 days later.

IN THE GARDEN

Of the three tit family members you are most likely to see in the garden, the coal tit is the smallest, the shyest and the most bullied. At feeders, it favours sunflower seeds, although all seed types and fat balls are eaten. To attract coal tits, place nest boxes – with small entrance holes – less than one metre from the ground.

MARSH TIT
Poecile palustris

LOOK/LISTEN FOR

Sneezy "pitchoo" call

•

Glossy black cap

•

Neat black bib

•

White cheeks

•

White undertail

•

Bluish legs

VOICE

You can see from the two photos here that marsh and willow tits are almost identical. The best way to tell them apart is by listening to their songs and calls. Marsh tits have a loud "pitchoo" call which sounds a bit like a squeaky toy or a sneeze, often followed by "chickabeebeebee", and its song is a rapidly repeated "chip-chip-chip". In contrast, the sound you are likely to hear a willow tit make is an angry-sounding "tchay" or "tchay-tchay-tchay" call.

NESTING

Deep down in a hole in a willow or alder tree is a likely spot for a marsh tit to build its mossy nest. The female sits tightly on her clutch of eggs for 13 days until they hatch, when the male helps to look after the young. About 18 days later, they are ready to fledge.

KEY FACTS

Found: *Large wooded gardens, mature woods, orchards*
Length: *12 cm*
Present: *January to December*
Food: *Seeds & insects*
Often seen: *On a perch*
Similar to: *Willow & coal tit*
Behaviour: *Bold*
Lives for: *Up to 11 years*
Nests: *In existing tree holes*
Eggs: *7 to 9 white eggs with red-brown speckles*
Broods: *1 per year*
Sexes: *Alike*
In UK: *England, Wales*

THE MARSH PART OF THIS BIRD'S NAME refers less to actual marshland and more to damp woods, especially ones with dense undergrowth where it likes to feed. In spring, the male sings to mark his territory and attract a mate. He then performs a courtship dance to seal the bond between them which will last for life. Sadly, this bird has seen a 53% decline in the last 25 years due to habitat loss.

IN THE GARDEN

Marsh tits favour large gardens with plenty of mature deciduous or dead trees where they can find holes in which to nest. Feeders are visited only when other food is scarce; the seeds will be taken away to eat elsewhere. Nest boxes are sometimes used if they face northwards and are close to the ground.

WILLOW TIT

Compared with marsh tits, willow tits have paler wing patches, duller caps and whiter cheeks. They also lack the white spot at the base of their upper beaks.

LONG-TAILED TIT
Aegithalos caudatus

KEY FACTS

Found: *Gardens, woods*
Length: *15 cm (including tail)*
Present: *January to December*
Food: *Insects & spiders*
Often seen: *In trees*
Similar to: *Nothing else*
Behaviour: *Sociable*
Lives for: *Up to 8 years*
Nests: *Low down in prickly bushes or high up in trees*
Eggs: *Up to 12 white eggs with red-brown freckles*
Broods: *1 per year*
Sexes: *Alike*
In UK: *Throughout*

LOOK/LISTEN FOR

Long tail
•
Tinkling flocks
•
Powder-pink undersides
•
Undulating flight
•
Tiny beak
•
Thick black eyebrow line
and white crown stripe

WITHOUT THE TAIL, this would be a very small fluffy ball of a bird. It is rare to see one on its own; it is most visible outside the breeding season when it roves around in flocks. Listen out for a tinkling chatter amongst the trees, which signals that they are in the area. This bird is not related to the true tits in the *Parus* family, though it is similar in being restless, sociable and acrobatic.

VOICE

The long-tailed tit's expertise lies more in nest-building than in musical performance. Unlike birds such as the robin, it uses its voice not to mark its territory but to maintain contact with other tits as it travels around. These flocks employ a range of sounds which send out information about food, location and danger. The most distinctive of these are a high-pitched "tsee-tsee-tsee" and a sharper "tsirrup". It is believed long-tailed tits can also recognise family members by their calls.

PARENTING

From February to July, the long-tailed tit is rarely seen as it concentrates on building its nest and raising its young – though the chicks are often snatched by larger birds and weasels. If this happens the adults sometimes help to feed the young of neighbouring pairs.

NEST

Among the thorny branches of a bush or high in a tree, long-tailed tits build cosy nests out of lichen, moss and cobwebs and line them with soft feathers.

IN THE GARDEN

Long-tailed tits usually visit feeders in the autumn and winter months, arriving hurriedly, feeding for a short time, then moving on. Such small birds struggle to survive freezing temperatures and may huddle together in old nest boxes to keep warm. These skilled nest-builders have no use for nest boxes for breeding.

HOUSE MARTIN
Delichon urbicum

LOOK/LISTEN FOR

White belly

•

Distinctive white rump

•

Shallow forked tail

•

Groups of cup-shaped mud nests under roof edges

•

Feathery white legs

•

Flocks soaring in the air

VOICE

House-martin colonies are noisy places where the air is filled with their constant chatter. They sing inside or by their nests as well as in flight. The sound is similar to a budgerigar's, with songs made up of long bubbling trills. In flight, they can also be heard making soft "prrt" calls to one another. Later on in summer, groups gather noisily on wires before they start migrating. It's fun to imagine them discussing which route to take...

MIGRATION

House martins arrive to breed in the spring from late March onwards. Once they have raised their young, birds begin to gather, often near fresh water, and by October, most have left. Little is known of where they spend the winter, but it is thought to be feeding on flying insects over the rainforests of central Africa.

YOU CAN SEE THE BLUE-BLACK colour of the house martin's head clearly in this picture. It looks similar to a swallow but its tail is shorter and less forked and it has a clear white patch on its rump. This summer visitor lives in colonies on the sides of buildings and spends much of its time in flight. It hunts for insects high in the air, coming to ground only to collect mud with which to build its nest.

KEY FACTS

Found: *Gardens, towns, some cities, lakes, cliffs*

Length: *12 cm*

Present: *March to October*

Food: *Insects*

Often seen: *Flying*

Similar to: *Swallow & swift*

Behaviour: *Sociable*

Lives for: *Up to 7 years*

Nests: *Under eaves of houses, river bridges or cliffs*

Eggs: *4 to 5 glossy white eggs*

Broods: *2 per year*

Sexes: *Alike*

In UK: *Throughout*

NEST

Both sexes craft the nest out of wet mud pellets bound with grass, leaving an entrance near the top. The nest is then lined with feathers before the eggs are laid.

IN THE GARDEN

House martins and sparrows both like to nest close to humans, although pollution and lack of mud for nest-building due to dryer springs have seen numbers fall. Putting up artificial cup-shaped nests under the eaves of your house is a good way to attract house martins, though sparrows may try to take them first.

WREN
Troglodytes troglodytes

KEY FACTS

Found: *Gardens, parks,
woods, farms*
Length: *10 cm*
Present: *January to December*
Food: *Insects*
Often seen: *Near the ground*
Similar to: *Nothing else*
Behaviour: *Secretive*
Lives for: *Up to 7 years*
Nests: *In holes in walls or trees*
Eggs: *5 to 6 buff white eggs
with reddish-brown freckles*
Broods: *2 per year*
Sexes: *Alike*
In UK: *Throughout*

NEST

The male may build up to 12 nests
from which a female will pick one,
at which point the nest will be
lined. There may be several females
nesting in the male's territory.

LOUD, LOWDOWN AND TINY – these are the main things to
remember about the wren which is one of our commonest
garden birds. It flits around the undergrowth in search
of small insects, often giving harsh "tchek" sounds when
alarmed. Its scientific name *troglodytes* means cave-dweller
from its habit of hiding away, which is also the reason it
is known in Iceland as "brother of the mouse".

IN THE GARDEN

Wrens are frequently found in gardens but are not visitors to bird
feeders except perhaps to pick nervously on the ground at dropped
seeds or mealworm. In mild winters, wrens roost alone at night but
when it is cold, groups often huddle together in nest boxes to keep
warm. Individuals call at dusk to attract others to join the roost.

LOOK/LISTEN FOR

Short upturned tail

•

"Tchek" alarm call coming
from the undergrowth

•

Reddish-brown upper parts
with barred wings

•

Loud high-pitched song
ending with a trill

•

Pale stripe over each eye

VOICE

From a low perch, the male
performs his warbling song with
gusto. He is one of the first to
sing in the dawn chorus and his
performance is made up of a series
of short bursts, each ending with
a trill. The song is so rapid, you
can hear only about 50 of the
740 notes he sings a minute. The
sound warns males to stay away,
while inviting females to come
and admire his nests. Listen out for
the wren's sharp "tchek" alarm call
when danger threatens.

PARENTING

The male wren is unusual in
having several mates. With the
need to build multiple nests and
with two broods per female a
year, in the breeding season he is
a busy bird. As a result, the female
is usually the one to incubate and
feed the chicks, which leave the
nest after 16 days.

GOLDCREST
Regulus regulus

LOOK/LISTEN FOR

Yellow crest (with orange
centre in males)

•

Greenish colouring

•

High-pitched twittering
sounds

•

Flitting around in upper
branches of fir trees

•

Thin, sharp, dark beak

VOICE

Walking among fir trees, you might become aware of tinkling notes from high up in the branches above you. These may be coming from a party of goldcrests busily foraging for insects and keeping in touch with one another using high-pitched "tsee-tsee-tsee" calls. In early spring, the male starts up his squeaky song, which sounds a bit like "diddly-dee" repeated up to five times and often ending with a different flourish. His song becomes more and more complex as the season progresses, reaching maximum force by April.

PARENTING

Even before the first brood has left the nest, the female may have laid another clutch of eggs. In this way, a single pair may raise up to 20 chicks a year. This helps to boost numbers after harsh winters, when goldcrest numbers often tumble.

THE SCIENTIFIC NAME *REGULUS* means king in Latin, which is appropriate given its golden crown but less so in terms of its size, for it is our smallest bird. Weighing about the same as five paperclips, this restless feathery bundle was once known as the golden-crested wren. Its mossy nest hangs like a tiny hammock from the branch of a conifer tree and is very hard to spot – which is the general idea.

IN THE GARDEN

Goldcrests come to bird feeders in the winter months when insects and spiders are hard to find. Autumn sees large numbers cross the North Sea from Russia and Scandinavia to join our resident birds and is when gardens on the east coast of Britain may be alive with these incomers before they move on.

KEY FACTS

Found: *Gardens, woods*
Length: *9 cm*
Present: *January to December*
Food: *Insects*
Often seen: *On a perch*
Similar to: *Firecrest*
Behaviour: *Secretive*
Lives for: *Up to 5 years*
Nests: *In conifer trees*
Eggs: *7 to 10 buff white eggs
with light brown markings*
Broods: *2 per year*
Sexes: *Male's crest becomes
more orange in breeding season*
In UK: *Throughout*

FIRECREST

Firecrests are slightly bigger than goldcrests, with white and black eye stripes. The crown of the female is yellow like the female goldcrest's, while the male's is a fiery orange.

BLACKCAP
Sylvia atricapilla

KEY FACTS

Habitat: *Gardens, parks, woodland edges*
Length: *Up to 13 cm*
Present: *January to December*
Food: *Flies, caterpillars & berries*
Often seen: *On a perch*
Similar to: *Marsh & willow tit*
Behaviour: *Shy*
Lives for: *Up to 10 years*
Nests: *In dense understorey*
Eggs: *4 to 5 beige marbled eggs*
Broods: *2 per year*
Sexes: *Female has chestnut cap*
In UK: *England, Wales*

LOOK/LISTEN FOR

Black cap (male)

•

Brown cap (female)

•

Musical warble

•

Hopping around in undergrowth

•

Overall grey colour

•

White eye crescent

THE BLACKCAP'S MUSICAL SONG is one of the finest of all, earning it the nickname "nightingale of the north". Although it can be heard clearly during the spring, it is less easy to spot once the leaves are out for it likes to stay hidden away in the undergrowth where it builds its delicate nest. In Germany, it is known as "the monk" because of its black or brown cap-like head feathers.

VOICE

When summer-visiting birds start to arrive here in April, the male blackcap joins in the dawn chorus in the hope of attracting a female and in order to defend his territory. His song starts gently and gradually becomes louder and clearer. Each verse is different from the last and may contain passages imitating other birds such as song thrushes and redstarts. The call is a very harsh "tchek" sound, repeated rapidly when the bird is alarmed.

WARBLERS

Blackcaps belong to a family of birds known as warblers. They are all small, insect-eating and particularly fine at singing. Most are browny-green in colour, making the blackcap one of the easiest to recognise. However, its song is very similar to that of the garden warbler except for being slightly slower and more varied.

FEMALE

The female has a chestnut cap and browner underparts and is slightly bigger than the male. Fledglings also have reddy-brown caps, which in males then become black.

IN THE GARDEN

Most of our blackcap population is made up of birds arriving in April to breed and leaving in October. Increasingly, some stay on during the winter months and are joined by migrants from central Europe. These winter blackcaps visit gardens to take peanuts and seeds at feeders, where they act aggressively towards other birds.

NUTHATCH
Sitta europaea

LOOK/LISTEN FOR

Climbing head first
down trees

•

Dagger-like grey beak

•

Pale orange breast

•

Black face line

•

Far-reaching trilling whistle

•

Hammering sound in trees

VOICE

A clear piping "pee-pee-pee" song ringing out through the trees signals the presence of a nuthatch. It sings from a high open perch to mark its territory and the only time it is really quiet is during the breeding season. It also has a wide range of calls, of which the most commonly heard is a clear "dweep" repeated two or more times, especially if the bird is alarmed.

DIET

In the autumn, if you hear a "tap-tap-tap" noise coming from a tree, it may be a nuthatch smashing nuts or large insects with its fearsome beak in the crevices of trees. It stores some of these for times when it is cold and food is scarce. The rest of the year, nuthatches feed on insects and their larvae. The male feeds the female to try and woo her and also when she is incubating her eggs.

KEY FACTS

Found: *Gardens, parks, woods*
Length: *14 cm*
Present: *January to December*
Food: *Insects, nuts & seeds*
Often seen: *Climbing up and down tree trunks*
Similar to: *Nothing else*
Behaviour: *Secretive*
Lives for: *Up to 10 years*
Nests: *In existing tree holes*
Eggs: *6 to 8 white eggs with red speckles*
Broods: *1 per year*
Sexes: *Male has darker breast*
In UK: *England, Wales*

ALTHOUGH THE NUTHATCH may be found in larger gardens, it is essentially a woodland bird, especially where there are oak and beech trees. It is much better at climbing than at flying and is famed for its ability to travel as easily head first down a tree as up it. Nuthatches form pairs for life. If you see two together, look for the male's slightly darker pinky-orange breast.

IN THE GARDEN

Armed with its lethal-looking beak and bandit-like eye stripe, the nuthatch swoops down to feeders, chases away smaller birds and then tucks in to any peanuts, sunflower seeds or suet on offer. There are long nesting boxes which these birds will use; they will often add mud to the entrance and insides.

NEST

The nuthatch makes its nest in an existing hole, especially one made by a woodpecker. It then plasters the entrance to make it smaller to prevent intruders from getting in.

TREECREEPER
Certhia familiaris

KEY FACTS

Found: *Gardens, woods*
Length: *13 cm*
Present: *January to December*
Food: *Insects & spiders*
Often seen: *Climbing trees from the base upwards*
Similar to: *Nothing else*
Behaviour: *Secretive*
Lives for: *Up to 8 years*
Nests: *In tree crevices or ivy*
Eggs: *3 to 8 white eggs with red-brown spots*
Broods: *2 per year*
Sexes: *Alike*
In UK: *Throughout*

UP OR DOWN?

Treecreepers and nuthatches are similar-sized birds with powerful claws for gripping, but where treecreepers climb *up* trunks, nuthatches often travel *down* them.

ONLY A FLASH OF ITS WHITE BREAST is likely to give the location of the treecreeper away, for its speckled brown back acts as the perfect camouflage against the mottled tree bark. Stiff tail feathers help to anchor it close to the trunk as it hops jerkily from the base upwards, picking out insects with its long curved beak. On reaching the top, the treecreeper flies down to the base of another tree.

IN THE GARDEN

There is not much you can do to attract treecreepers to your garden. They are shy and rarely visit bird tables or use nest boxes, though some success has been had with wedge-shaped boxes with open backs. You could try pasting suet and seed mixture onto tree trunks as an additional food supply in the winter.

LOOK/LISTEN FOR

Climbing up a tree, then flying to the base of another

•

Speckled brown back and bright white breast

•

Long, curved beak

•

Very high call with single note being repeated

•

Pointed tail tips

VOICE

You may hear the treecreeper's soft high-pitched "see-see-see" sound as it makes its way up a tree or flies from one tree to another. Its song is shrill and more warbling than its calls and gets rapidly faster until it ends with a flourish. The male sings in the spring to attract a female with whom he will raise one or two broods.

NESTING

Treecreepers build their nests from late March behind loose pieces of tree bark, in cracks or splits in trunks or in amongst ivy – places where there hardly seems to be enough room. The only clue to its presence may be some grass or straw poking out of a crack. The female lines the nest with feathers and wool before laying the eggs. The adults raise up to eight chicks which are ready to fledge after around two weeks.

WAXWING
Bombycilla garrulus

LOOK/LISTEN FOR

Punky crest

•

Black bib & mask

•

Yellow wing & tail tips

•

Chestnut undertail

•

Sudden flocks in berried
trees during the winter

•

Trilling call

VOICE

One of the main reasons birds sing,
particularly males, is to defend
their territory. Waxwings are
unusual in that they don't have
territories, which is probably why
they have no distinct song. Instead,
the noise they make is a rapid
high-pitched trill, which some say
sounds like sleigh bells.

DIET

Food is more important to a
waxwing than just as something
to keep it alive. The colour from
the berries it eats contributes to
the yellow and red of its wings
and tail feathers as they are
growing. Older waxwings have
an increased number and area
of coloured feathers. Food is also
used in waxwing courtship, for
newly formed male and female
pairs will pass food between each
other up to 14 times to cement
their relationship.

IT SEEMS SLIGHTLY ODD that this bird was named after
the rather hard-to-spot waxy red wing tips and not its
incredible crest or striking black mask. It is an exotic-
looking bird which arrives in the autumn from breeding
grounds near the Arctic Circle in search of food. There
may be a few hundred or, if the berry crop is poor on
mainland Europe, they may come in their thousands.

KEY FACTS

Found: *Open country,
gardens, towns*
Length: *18 cm*
Present: *November to March*
Food: *Berries*
Often seen: *In trees*
Similar to: *Nothing else*
Behaviour: *Sociable*
Lives for: *Up to 3 years*
Nests: *In trees*
Eggs: *6 spotted lilac eggs*
(note: it doesn't breed in UK)
Broods: *1 per year*
Sexes: *Male greyer*
In UK: *Mainly north & east*

WAXWING FLOCKS

The *garrulus* part of this bird's
scientific name means talkative or
sociable – a good description of
these noisy flocks. They rest in trees
when not stripping them of berries.

IN THE GARDEN

The best way to tempt waxwings to your garden is to plant trees
that droop with berries in the late autumn and winter, such as
rowans and hawthorns. Even this does not ensure success, for
waxwings roam like nomads from one place to another and it is
impossible to predict where or when you will see them.

STARLING
Sturnus vulgaris

KEY FACTS

Found: *Gardens, farms,
towns, cities*
Length: *22 cm*
Present: *January to December*
Food: *Insects, seeds & berries*
Often seen: *On the ground*
Similar to: *Blackbird*
Behaviour: *Sociable*
Lives for: *Up to 17 years*
Nests: *In holes in roofs or trees*
Eggs: *4 to 5 pale blue eggs*
Broods: *Mostly 1 per year*
Sexes: *Female has pink bill
base, male blue when breeding*
In UK: *Throughout*

LOOK/LISTEN FOR

Spotted appearance
in winter

•

Long, pointed bill
(yellow in breeding season)

•

Short tail

•

Iridescent feathers

•

Huge cloud-like flocks in the
autumn and winter

THE JERKY WALK OF THE STARLING as it patrols the lawn is very different from the sight of it flying purposefully through the sky. As it flies, you can see the triangular shape of its wings as well as its short tail. In spring, the male builds an untidy nest and sings to attract a female. She will complete the nest by lining it with feathers and grass before laying her pale blue eggs in it.

VOICE

The starling is a good mimic and can make noises that sound like other animals or mechanical devices. It is a noisy bird and, in winter flocks, chatters away busily on chimney pots and wires or in trees. In the spring, individuals leave the flocks to breed and each male begins his whistling, clicking and trilling songs to attract a mate.

COLOURING

Young starlings are a pale brown colour and are quite unlike their black glossy parents. During the winter, the adults have whitish flecks all over them, and their beaks and legs are dark in colour like those of the bird you can see here. In the spring, their beaks turn yellow and their legs become a pinker colour, while the spots on their feathers fade away. At all times, their feathers shine with tints of green, blue and purple.

MURMURATIONS

In the autumn, huge flocks known as murmurations gather at dusk, in cities and reedbeds, to roost. Up to a million birds swirl around the sky before settling for the night.

IN THE GARDEN

The only other garden bird similar to the starling is the blackbird. If you look at the bird opposite, you can see that its bill is wider than the starling's and its feathers have no obvious speckles. Both birds look for food on the ground, but while the blackbird moves by hopping, the starling walks.

BLACKBIRD
Turdus merula

LOOK/LISTEN FOR

Male's golden yellow beak and yellow eye ring

•

Melodious song delivered from high perches

•

Explosive squawk if disturbed

•

Tail raising as it perches

•

Hopping around on lawns

VOICE

Males start singing from a high perch on sunny days in late winter. Each male develops his own flute-like song which gets more elaborate as the breeding season progresses, but by July his song is over. Adult blackbirds make an array of other sounds to signal alarm, aggression and excitement, while chicks have a special call for demanding food.

NESTING

Blackbird pairs look for suitable nest sites in early spring in dense undergrowth such as evergreen shrubs. Once their sturdy nest has been built, the female lays one egg a morning until her clutch is complete. On hatching, the chicks grow fast and are ready to leave the nest after 13 days. Unlike most birds, the adults divide their fledglings into two groups and look after one half each.

KEY FACTS

Found: *Gardens, woods, towns*
Length: *25 cm*
Present: *January to December*
Food: *Worms, insects & berries*
Often seen: *On the ground*
Similar to: *Starling*
Behaviour: *Bold*
Lives for: *Up to 14 years*
Nests: *In cup near the ground in undergrowth*
Eggs: *4 or 5 light blue eggs with spots*
Broods: *2 to 3 per year*
Sexes: *Female is brown*
In UK: *Throughout*

THIS WAS ONCE A SHY WOODLAND BIRD, but the early 20th century saw the successful spread of blackbirds into towns and cities. What you think of as your garden is probably the territory of a breeding pair who fiercely patrol and defend their borders against intruders – especially other blackbirds and thrushes. New pairs form in the early spring and will stay together until one of them dies.

IN THE GARDEN

This is one of our most popular garden birds, loved for its flute-like song. It hops about garden lawns before pulling earthworms from the soil. In colder months, it relies on berries too as a food source to keep it alive. This is a good time to help by leaving out fruit or mealworms on the ground for them to feed on.

FEMALE

The female is not black but dark brown, with a slightly speckled chest and darker bill. Occasionally, blackbirds with patches of white feathers have been recorded.

SONG THRUSH
Turdus philomelos

LOOK/LISTEN FOR

Arrowhead spots

•

Orange underwing

•

White eye ring &
pale pink legs

•

Singing from an open perch

•

Running along lawns

•

Fledglings in early spring

KEY FACTS

Found: *Gardens, parks, woods*
Length: *23 cm*
Present: *January to December*
Food: *Insects, worms,
snails & berries*
Often seen: *On the ground*
Similar to: *Mistle thrush,
redwing & fieldfare*
Behaviour: *Shy*
Lives for: *Up to 11 years*
Nests: *In hedges, trees or bushes*
Eggs: *4 to 5 spotted blue eggs*
Broods: *2 to 3 per year*
Sexes: *Alike*
In UK: *Throughout*

HOP, RUN, HEAD TURN ... then, if it is lucky, the song thrush will draw an unsuspecting worm from the ground. It forages for food staying close to the undergrowth in which it may build a cup-shaped nest lined with soft mud and smoothed by the female's breast. This thrush is one of our most skilled and melodious songbirds; its population has more than halved since the 1970s.

VOICE

This is one of the easiest bird songs to learn, for the male repeats each phrase up to five times. The sound is loud and clear, particularly at dusk when few other birds are singing. The male delivers his performance from an open perch from as early as January, especially if the weather is fine. His song becomes increasingly complex and may contain notes mimicking birds such as nuthatches or owls and sometimes machinery. If alarmed, it makes a "tchuk-tchuk" call.

PREENING

The song thrush spends more time than many birds attending to personal hygiene – bathing in puddles, preening its feathers and even sunbathing. Once a year, it also goes through an annual moult, gradually shedding and regrowing its feathers. This takes about 50 days from July to September.

FLEDGLING

You may see young song thrushes as early as the end of March, for the adults are quick to nest in the spring. The fledglings look like the parents but have spottier backs.

IN THE GARDEN

Gardens with lawns and shrubs are favoured as they provide food and nesting sites. At feeding stations, song thrushes will eat mealworms, fruit or peck at dropped seeds. If you happen to find fragments of shell, it may be the result of the song thrush's habit of smashing snails against stones to reach their juicy insides.

MISTLE THRUSH
Turdus viscivorus

LOOK/LISTEN FOR

Speckled breast

•

White underwings

•

Singing in all weathers

•

Upright stance

•

Pale outer tail feathers

•

Pale rump

VOICE

If you hear a loud song that has the same flute-like notes as a blackbird's but with shorter phrases and longer pauses, then you might be listening to a mistle thrush. It delivers its song from the top of a tall tree within its territory. Its alarm call is made up of a forceful rapid-fire series of notes.

SONG OR MISTLE?

The mistle thrush is very similar to the song thrush except that:
• it is bigger, greyer, stands taller on the ground and also flies higher.
• its chest is paler and its outer tail feathers have white tips to them.
• the feathers under its wings are almost white, while those of the song thrush are orangey-brown.
• its spots are bolder and rounded, while the song thrush's are notched like arrowheads.
• its song lacks the repeated phrases of the song thrush's.

KEY FACTS

Found: *Gardens, parks, woodland edges*
Length: *27 cm*
Present: *January to December*
Food: *Fruit, berries & worms*
Often seen: *On the ground*
Similar to: *Song thrush, fieldfare & redwing*
Behaviour: *Shy*
Lives for: *Up to 11 years*
Nests: *In forks of trees*
Eggs: *4 speckled eggs*
Broods: *2 per year*
Sexes: *Alike*
In UK: *Throughout*

THIS FIESTY THRUSH WILL SING from late winter to June even if the weather is bad, which is how it came by the name of storm-cock. Boldly, it will fight any intruders intent on stealing its chicks or food within its territory. Once the breeding season is over, groups of mistle thrushes roam the countryside in search of food, and in the autumn they are joined by visitors from other parts of Europe.

IN THE GARDEN

If you have a large garden with tall trees, you may be lucky enough to have a pair of mistle thrushes in residence. Their territories are larger than those of the blackbird or song thrush so you are unlikely to have more than a pair in one garden. Its favourite berries are mistletoe (hence its name), yew, holly and ivy.

NEST

Hidden away among the branches of trees such as yew and elder, the mistle thrush's nest is made out of sticks, moss and roots, reinforced with mud and lined with grass.

FIELDFARE
Turdus pilaris

KEY FACTS

Found: *Gardens, farms, hedges*
Length: *26 cm*
Present: *October to April*
Food: *Berries and worms*
Often seen: *In flocks in trees*
Similar to: *Mistle thrush*
Behaviour: *Sociable*
Lives for: *Up to 14 years*
Nests: *Small trees, ground*
Eggs: *4 to 7 blue-green eggs*
(note: it doesn't breed in UK)
Broods: *2 per year*
Sexes: *Female is paler*
In UK: *Throughout*

LOOK/LISTEN FOR

Foraging in flocks

•

"Chack-chack-chack" call

•

Chevroned sides

•

Pale grey rump and white
underwings visible in flight

•

Long black tail and dark legs

•

Orange chest

FIELDFARES MAKE THEIR WAY ACROSS the North Sea in the autumn arriving here from parts of northern Europe where winters are extremely harsh. They scour the countryside in flocks – sometimes in their hundreds – searching noisily for food and roosting together at night in order to stay warm. They return to northern breeding grounds in spring where they nest in colonies.

VOICE

Some thrushes, such as the song thrush and the blackbird, are famed for their musical singing. The fieldfare's song is loud but the notes it makes are harsh, buzzy and mechanical rather than tuneful. Its loud chattering may be the first thing you are aware of when a flock enters your neighbourhood or is passing overhead.

THE THRUSH FAMILY

There are over 60 different species of thrush found throughout the world; most of them are plump, inquisitive birds. Their nests are sturdy, cup-shaped and often lined with mud where they lay three to six blue-green eggs. Most thrushes eat fruit, insects and worms and some thrush species migrate south during the winter in order to find food in warmer countries.

SEASONAL FOOD

Pictures of fieldfares often show them in winter feasting on berries. In the summer, their diet changes to insects, worms and snails.

IN THE GARDEN

It is hard to predict when and where you will see these winter visitors. Fieldfares do not return to the same wintering grounds but wander at random wherever food is available. The chances that they will venture into your garden increase if you grow shrubs that produce autumn berries and if you leave out chopped apples.

REDWING
Turdus iliacus

LOOK/LISTEN FOR

Pale stripe over the eyes

•

Orange-red underwings

•

Yellow and black beak

•

Striped breast

•

Sudden flocks appearing in winter and then going

•

High-pitched flight call

VOICE

On fine days in early spring, flocks of redwings may be heard chattering. The male's full song – several clear notes followed by an extended burbling trill – may be heard in the birch and conifer forests in northern Europe where it breeds. In alarm, a shrill "tchek" call is given which is similar to that of the wren.

MIGRATION

At night-time in October, you may hear the soft, high-pitched "seep" sound given by flocks of migrating redwings as they pass overhead. Their journeys began in the forests of Scandinavia and Russia and they may have flown as many as 4,000 miles in search of milder winter temperatures in other parts of Europe, North Africa and the Middle East. These birds are some of the first to perish in bad weather.

KEY FACTS

Found: *Gardens, meadows*
Length: *22 cm*
Present: *October to April*
Food: *Berries and worms*
Often seen: *On the ground*
Similar to: *Song thrush*
Behaviour: *Sociable*
Lives for: *Up to 11 years*
Nests: *Bushes, trees, ground*
Eggs: *4 to 6 blue speckled eggs*
(note: it doesn't breed in UK)
Broods: *2 per year*
Sexes: *Female is paler*
In UK: *Throughout*

THIS, OUR SMALLEST THRUSH, is a winter visitor and is in the UK only between the months of October and April. It roams in loose flocks, sometimes with fieldfares, blackbirds and starlings, travelling nomadically in search of food. When a flock is feeding, one bird acts as a look-out at the top of a nearby tall tree. At the first whiff of danger, the sentinel sends out a cry of alarm and the flock disperses.

IN THE GARDEN

Redwings, like all thrushes, eat berries, but their main diet consists of insects, snails, worms and some fruit. They usually visit gardens only when freezing weather makes other food sources scarce, when they may be quite tame. Plant rowans, hawthorns and apple trees to attract redwings – but don't expect them to stay long.

COLOURING

Although the redwing looks similar to the song thrush, the markings on its chest are more like dashes than spots. Look out for the distinctive orangey red colour under its wings.

ROBIN
Erithacus rubecula

KEY FACTS

Found: *Gardens, farms, towns, woodland*
Length: *14 cm*
Present: *January to December*
Food: *Insects, snails and worms*
Often seen: *On a perch*
Similar to: *Nothing else*
Behaviour: *Bold*
Lives for: *Up to 8 years*
Nests: *Near the ground*
Eggs: *3 to 6 white spotted eggs*
Broods: *2 per year*
Sexes: *Alike*
In UK: *Throughout*

LOOK/LISTEN FOR

Red face and breast
•
Tail twitching and bobbing
up and down
•
Droopy wings
•
White belly and undertail
•
Long legs
•
Ticking call

VOICE

From a high perch, the robin delivers its clear, piping song. This is made up of ever-changing musical phrases, lasting up to three seconds with pauses in between. Both male and female sing to defend their territories in the winter but only the male sings in the spring. When anxious, robins deliver a volley of rapid "tik-tik" sounds.

DAWN CHORUS

The dawn chorus begins in the spring with the start of the breeding season and reaches a peak by mid-May. Even before sunrise, male birds fill the air with song to attract a mate and defend their territory. The robin joins in about 50 minutes before sunrise. It is also one of the last to sing in the evening and may even be confused into singing through the night if there are street lights on.

WITH ITS BRIGHT BLACK EYES, unmistakable orange breast and rounded head, the robin keeps watch over its garden patch. If another robin dares to invade this space – apart from a potential mate – it will be attacked. In the UK, robins are bold birds happy to breed near humans, yet on the continent they are shyer creatures more commonly seen in woodlands than in gardens.

FLEDGLING

This fledgling is losing its first speckled brown feathers to reveal a smart red bib. The earlier drab colours help to keep the chicks safe.

IN THE GARDEN

In the breeding season, most gardens are home to a pair of robins; in the autumn, the female usually moves away to establish her own territory. Robins feed from flat bird tables, will take most foods and are especially fond of mealworms. They may use an open-fronted nest box if you hide it away in ivy.

SPOTTED FLYCATCHER
Muscicapa striata

LOOK/LISTEN FOR

Grey-brown upperparts

•

Pale streaked underparts

•

Streaked crown

•

Long wings

•

Sudden flight from a low perch in pursuit of an insect

•

Upright stance

VOICE

The spotted flycatcher certainly wouldn't win first prize in a muscial competition. The male sings on arrival in May to mark his territory and to lure a female. The sound to our ears is faint and unremarkable and consists of high notes delivered at intervals with a few squiggly buzzes and trills added in – more like a call than a song. Easier to hear is the loud "chack" that flycatchers make when they are anxious or alarmed.

CATCHING INSECTS

The scientific name of this slender bird is *Muscicapa striata*. Translated from Latin, *musca* means fly, *capere* is to capture and *striatus* means streaked. As a capturer of flies, it excels. Keep a look-out for one darting out from a low perch, twisting and turning after its prey, until, with a loud snap, its beak closes around it.

ARRIVING FROM AFRICA in May, this is one of the last summer visitors to reach us. Flycatcher numbers have been declining for many years because of falling numbers of insects and loss of habitat in both their wintering and their breeding grounds. Though they eat mostly flies, they will take stinging insects, too, which they rub against their perches to remove the sting before eating them.

KEY FACTS

Found: *Gardens, parks woodland*

Length: *14 cm*

Present: *May to October*

Food: *Insects*

Often seen: *On a perch*

Similar to: *Nothing else*

Behaviour: *Secretive*

Lives for: *Up to 8 years*

Nests: *Walls and ledges*

Eggs: *4 to 5 spotted green eggs*

Broods: *1 to 2 per year*

Sexes: *Alike*

In UK: *Throughout*

NESTING

The female makes her small nest out of moss and lichen and lines it with hair and feathers. She lays her eggs in May, often raising a second brood before the end of August.

IN THE GARDEN

You may not be aware of a flycatcher in your garden as it is a dull-coloured bird with no distinctive song and inclined to be secretive when breeding. Females have been known to occupy north-facing nest boxes with open fronts, and growing creepers such as ivy will help to create natural nest sites for them, too.

HOUSE SPARROW
Passer domesticus

KEY FACTS

Found: *Gardens, farms, towns*
Length: *14 cm*
Present: *January to December*
Food: *Seeds and insects*
Often seen: *On a perch*
Similar to: *Dunnock,
tree sparrow*
Behaviour: *Sociable*
Lives for: *Up to 12 years*
Nests: *Holes in roofs, hedges*
Eggs: *4 to 5 pale speckled eggs*
Broods: *2 to 3 per year*
Sexes: *Female is plainer*
In UK: *Throughout*

FEW BIRDS LIVE QUITE AS CLOSE to humans as house sparrows. Rather than having individual territories, sparrows live in colonies where life seems to be always noisy and busy. The males with the largest black throat patches are usually dominant, and during the breeding season their thick beaks change from a light brown colour, like the female's, to black as shown above.

FEMALE

You can see here the lighter colouring of the female compared with the male in the main picture. She has no black bib and she is also slightly smaller.

IN THE GARDEN

Sparrows feed on seeds, peanuts and suet, especially if there is a hedge nearby to protect them. They are a common sight near outside eating areas, where they hop around searching for scraps. Putting up several nest boxes may attract a colony, though it could take a while for them to be found as sparrows rarely roam far.

LOOK/LISTEN FOR

Grey crown, cheeks and
black bib (male)

•

Small wing bar

•

Thick, conical beak

•

Hopping hopefully around
picnic tables and cafés

•

Groups chattering in
hedgerows

VOICE

Many hedges seem to be alive with the chatter of sparrows in the spring and summer. This cheery sound is composed of a string of chirps and cheeps that seem to have no beginning or end. The male's tuneless song is an extended series of call notes which he uses to announce the fact that he has a nest and to attract a female to it. When alarmed, sparrows make a loud, rattling, churring sound.

COLONIES

House-sparrow numbers have been falling for many years, which may seem hard to believe if you have a noisy colony living near you. They build their nests under roof edges or take over old ones belonging to house martins. You can tell if this has happened by the bits of straw sticking out of the nests. A pair of sparrows may produce up to 18 chicks in one year.

DUNNOCK
Prunella modularis

LOOK/LISTEN FOR

Musical song

•

Blue-grey throat

•

Striped back and sides

•

Thin dark beak

•

Pink legs

•

Male singing on a perch
from October to July

VOICE

Most birds find their voice in the spring during the breeding season, but dunnocks sing from October through to July when they disappear to moult. The male performs his sweet, high-pitched warbling song from an open perch. The sound could be mistaken for a wren's but it is less musical and lacks the wren's distinctive trilling. A high piping "tseep" call is used when dunnocks are alarmed.

BREEDING

Unlike some bird species which form pairs for life, the dunnock is a bit more relaxed on the mating front. Both the male and the female may have several partners, and the chicks in a single brood may be fathered by different males. One reason for this is that male dunnocks sometimes have overlapping territories.

KEY FACTS

Found: *Gardens, hedges, towns*
Length: *Up to 15 cm*
Present: *January to December*
Food: *Insects, spiders, worms and seeds*
Often seen: *On the ground*
Similar to: *House sparrow*
Behaviour: *Shy*
Lives for: *Up to 11 years*
Nests: *Low in bushes or hedges*
Eggs: *4 to 5 turquoise eggs*
Broods: *2 per year*
Sexes: *Alike*
In UK: *Throughout*

EVEN THOUGH MOST GARDENS are home to a breeding pair of dunnocks, it is one of our least-known common birds. It is probably its habit of creeping about secretively at the bottom of bushes, and the fact that its feathers are an unexciting brown colour, that cause the dunnock to fall under most people's bird radar. It used to be known as a hedge sparrow but it is no relation to the species opposite.

IN THE GARDEN

Nest boxes are not for dunnocks – they build their nests low down in tangled undergrowth where they lay four or five bright blue eggs. Their use of feeding stations is sparing, though they may shuffle around at the base of bird feeders picking up crumbs and fallen seeds, especially in winter.

CUCKOO

Cuckoos often select dunnock nests in which to lay a single egg. On hatching, the cuckoo pushes out any other eggs or chicks and the adults raise it as their own.

PIED WAGTAIL
Motacilla alba yarrellii

KEY FACTS

Found: *Gardens, farms, towns*
Length: *18 cm*
Present: *January to December*
Food: *Mostly insects*
Often seen: *On the ground*
Similar to: *Nothing else*
Behaviour: *Timid*
Lives for: *Up to 11 years*
Nests: *Cavities in walls and buildings*
Eggs: *5 speckled grey eggs*
Broods: *2 per year*
Sexes: *Female is greyer*
In UK: *Throughout*

THESE SMALL BLACK-AND-WHITE birds walk hurriedly along the ground or the ridge of a house before stopping to bob, look round in case of danger, and then move on. Though nervous, they are happy to live near humans, making their nests in the nooks and crannies of old buildings. In the autumn, wagtails travel around in flocks when hundreds may roost together at night.

LOOK/LISTEN FOR

Long, bobbing tail
•
White face and black bib
•
Long legs
•
Quick running movements
•
Undulating flight
•
Loud two-note "chis-wick" flight call

VOICE

The excited twittering song of the pied wagtail is hard to make out in the noisy air of springtime. More instantly recognisable is its shrill two-note "chis-wick" flight call. This sound is uttered by the male when he is courting a female. He calls to her while lowering his head, dropping his wings and fanning out his tail.

WHITE WAGTAIL

The pied wagtail is a darker version (subspecies) of the white wagtail which is more commonly found in continental Europe. It is easier to tell the difference between them in the spring when the pied wagtail is much blacker. Once the birds have gone through a complete moult in the autumn, trying to identify the sex and species of these wagtails can be quite tricky.

GREY WAGTAIL

It is called grey, but this wagtail is striking for its soft lemon underparts. It has a longer tail and shorter legs than the pied wagtail and is found by rivers.

IN THE GARDEN

In spring, you may find male pied wagtails attacking their reflections in your windows, believing they have seen a rival. Nesting pairs are easy to spot as they patrol the surrounding area before taking food to their young. Growing creepers such as ivy is a good way to provide a rich source of flies for hungry wagtails.

CHAFFINCH

Fringilla coelebs

LOOK/LISTEN FOR

Flashes of white on the wings and tail in flight

•

Pink breast and blue-grey crown (male)

•

"Pink-pink" alarm call

•

Male singing high up in a tree almost continually in the spring

VOICE

The cascading song of the chaffinch is a familiar sound from February through to June. However, you might not know what bird is singing, for the male is often hard to spot at the tops of trees. Each burst lasts for two to three seconds and ends with a flourish followed by a pause, and then another burst begins. This is continued throughout spring, with unpaired males singing every seven to 15 seconds. Interestingly, chaffinches are known to have different "accents" according to the regions they come from.

NESTING

Like the long-tailed tit, the nest of the chaffinch is beautifully constructed of moss and wool and decorated with lichen for camouflage. Inside, a soft, downy lining of hair and feathers is made on which the eggs are laid.

KEY FACTS

Found: *Gardens, farms, woods*
Length: *Up to 14.5 cm*
Present: *January to December*
Food: *Seeds and insects*
Often seen: *On the ground*
Similar to: *Brambling, bullfinch*
Behaviour: *Shy*
Lives for: *Up to 13 years*
Nests: *In bushes or small trees*
Eggs: *4 to 5 speckled blue eggs*
Broods: *1 per year*
Sexes: *Female olive-brown*
In UK: *Throughout*

THIS POPULAR GARDEN BIRD is our commonest finch. It sings its way through spring until pairs have bred and individuals join loose groups for the autumn and winter. The scientific name *coelebs* means unmarried or single and refers to the fact that many of these flocks are made up of either males or females. Like pied wagtails, chaffinches will attack their own reflection in windows.

FEMALE

Females and juvenile chaffinches are much paler than males, though they still have the white wing bars and tail feathers visible when they fly.

IN THE GARDEN

Chaffinches are some of the first birds in the year to breed and their nests may be visible even before the leaves are fully out on the trees. Take care, for they are sensitive to being watched while they nest-build which can result in the nests' being deserted. At feeders, groups often pick around at spilled seeds on the ground.

BRAMBLING
Fringilla montifringilla

KEY FACTS

Found: *Gardens, woodland*
Length: *15 cm*
Present: *October to April*
Food: *Seeds, some insects*
Often seen: *On the ground*
Similar to: *Chaffinch*
Behaviour: *Shy*
Lives for: *Up to 8 years*
Nests: *Forks of trees*
Eggs: *5 to 7 greenish eggs*
(note: it doesn't breed in UK)
Broods: *1 per year*
Sexes: *Female is browner*
In UK: *Throughout*

LOOK/LISTEN FOR

Yellow beak except for black
bill of male when breeding

•

Orange shoulder and breast
(male colouring)

•

White rump visible in flight

•

Nasal call

•

Flocks gathered on forest
floors under beech trees

THIS COLOURFUL BIRD is a winter visitor that arrives from September and is gone by the end of April. Its breeding grounds lie in the far north of Europe among birch trees and conifers where it raises one brood. This male brambling is in its winter plumage; its head and beak will turn black in the breeding season. The female is much paler than this and looks more like a hen chaffinch.

VOICE

This is not the most tuneful garden bird. Some of its calls have a buzzy mechanical edge to them, rather like the "dzwee" sound of the greenfinch or the churring noises that some night-time animals make. Large roosting flocks or birds on migration can create quite a din as they keep in constant contact with one another. The male's song is a rasping, long-drawn-out note slowly repeated. This can be heard from March before it leaves for its breeding grounds.

MIGRATION

The number of bramblings reaching the UK each winter depends on the severity of the weather and the amount of food available in their breeding grounds. In harsh winters, more bramblings arrive here hoping to escape freezing conditions abroad.

FLOCKS

You may see huge flocks of bramblings in the winter, often mixed in with chaffinches which they closely resemble. They scour forests in search of beechmast.

IN THE GARDEN

Bramblings are infrequent garden visitors and if they do appear it may be in large numbers. They will eat from hanging feeders but prefer to peck around on the ground or at low bird tables – especially if you put out sunflower seeds or mealworms. A regular supply of fresh water is also important – for all garden birds.

GREENFINCH

Chloris chloris

LOOK/LISTEN FOR

Solid bird with large head

•

Thick, pale pink bill

•

Yellow wing edges

•

Forked tail

•

Male is strikingly green

•

Twittering, buzzy song

VOICE

The male greenfinch delivers his song made up of trills and warbles from favourite spots at the tops of trees. He also performs a special song flight: this involves circling around in the sky with wings beating slowly while he makes a light, tinny, chattering sound, often with a buzzy "dzwee" note mixed in. In fact, it is this buzzy twist to the song that marks it out as a greenfinch. These garden birds will continue to sing into July when most others are quiet.

NESTING

This sociable bird often builds its straggly nest near other greenfinches in hedges and trees, where pairs rear between four and six chicks. There may be two broods in a season, starting at the end of April or early May. The young hatch after two weeks and fledge 13 days after that.

THE GREENFINCH IS A SERIOUS-LOOKING BIRD with a thick, seed-cracking pink beak and large dark eyes. It is resident throughout the year, though some birds may migrate south in winter. Those that stay are often seen in flocks with other finches roaming the countryside in search of food. Greenfinch numbers have crashed since 2009 owing to the spread of a disease called trichomonosis.

IN THE GARDEN

A flash of vivid green may catch your eye as this stocky bird descends to take charge at a bird feeder. Here it fights off rivals to make sure it gets enough food, with sunflower seeds being a favourite. Cleaning feeders regularly helps to prevent birds from catching diseases; this is vitally important for greenfinches.

KEY FACTS

Found: *Gardens, farms, hedgerows*
Length: *Up to 15 cm*
Present: *January to December*
Food: *Seeds, fruit, nuts, insects*
Often seen: *On a perch*
Similar to: *Siskin*
Behaviour: *Bold*
Lives for: *Up to 12 years*
Nests: *In hedges and trees*
Eggs: *4 to 6 white spotted eggs*
Broods: *2 per year*
Sexes: *Female is browner*
In UK: *Throughout*

FEMALE

The female is smaller and paler than the male. She has faint streaks on her back and, like the male, has yellow wing edges which are visible in flight.

GOLDFINCH

Carduelis carduelis

KEY FACTS

Found: *Gardens, farmland, hedgerows*
Length: *Up to 12 cm*
Present: *January to December*
Food: *Small seeds, fruit, insects*
Often seen: *On a perch*
Similar to: *Nothing else*
Behaviour: *Sociable*
Lives for: *Up to 10 years*
Nests: *In trees, shrubs, bushes*
Eggs: *4 to 6 blue speckled eggs*
Broods: *2 per year*
Sexes: *Alike*
In UK: *Throughout*

THE GOLDFINCH IS AN UNMISTAKABLE garden visitor with a masked red face, flashing yellow wing feathers and bouncing flight style. The adults are alike, but the young don't get their red faces until the autumn of their first year. Goldfinch numbers were once threatened as a result of the fashion for keeping them as tuneful caged birds, but this practice was banned and numbers now are strong.

LOOK/LISTEN FOR

Red face
•
Yellow wing bars
•
White rump
•
Spotted tail feathers
•
Chattering flight call
•
Flocks feeding on seedheads in autumn and winter

VOICE

The goldfinch is a noisy bird which can be heard throughout the year. The male delivers his high-pitched twittering song from a suitable perch in order to attract a mate. Outside the breeding season, flocks of goldfinches call out regularly to one another – both in flight and at rest – with a tinkling chattering sound with raspy elements to it.

CHARMS

Once the time for rearing chicks is over, goldfinches gather in flocks called charms. Together, they scour farmland and wasteland for plants that produce small seeds such as thistles, teasels and burdocks. A large number of goldfinches fly south to avoid the deep cold of winter, returning in February or March to breed.

NEST

Its tidy nest of roots, grass and moss, lined with hair and feathers, is made in fruit trees or hidden in climbing shrubs. Two or three broods are produced between May and August, with both parents raising their young.

IN THE GARDEN

Putting out niger or sunflower seeds is a good way of encouraging goldfinches into your garden. They may look attractive but the same cannot be said for their manners. They regularly squabble amongst themselves in order to reach any available seed and are pretty forceful in shooing away other hopeful diners.

SISKIN

Spinus spinus

LOOK/LISTEN FOR

Black crown and chin (male)

•

Short, clearly forked tail

•

Lemony yellow wing bars, rump and tail edges

•

Streaked sides

•

Twittery trilling song

•

Seen mostly in winter

VOICE

Like goldfinches, siskins used to be kept as caged songbirds prized for their sweet warbling songs. Nowadays, their high "speeoo" call is heard only in the wild. In the spring, the male selects an open perch and tries to impress nearby females with bursts of whistles, warbles and trills. In winter, the contact calls between birds in flocks are almost constant.

NESTING

Spotting the nests of siskins is difficult as they build them high up in the branches of conifers, such spruces, silver firs and Scots pines. The tiny cup-shaped nest is made with a mixture of moss, twigs, lichen, wool and feathers. Eggs are laid from April to June with the chicks hatching after about 12 days. They are fed on small insects and after 15 days are ready to leave the nest.

KEY FACTS

Found: *Gardens, riversides, parks, woodland*
Length: *12 cm*
Present: *January to December*
Food: *Seeds*
Often seen: *High in conifers*
Similar to: *Greenfinch*
Behaviour: *Sociable*
Lives for: *Up to 8 years*
Nests: *In trees*
Eggs: *4 to 5 blue blotchy eggs*
Broods: *2 per year*
Sexes: *Female is paler*
In UK: *Throughout*

THE SISKIN IS A SMALL, restless bird, constantly on the move in search of food. It hangs blue-tit-like from alder and birch branches especially near water, feeding on seeds using its pointed bill. In the autumn, siskins that spend all year here are joined by winter migrants fleeing the cold on the continent. They often form large chattering flocks with redpolls, with which they have been known to breed.

FEMALE

The female lacks the black head and chin of the male and is paler, with grey streaks on her undersides. Juveniles are browner.

IN THE GARDEN

Flocks of siskins usually visit gardens only during the winter months when food elsewhere is in short supply. Their preference is for niger seeds, sunflower hearts and peanuts – but don't expect them to stay long. Though they generally nest in woodland they may use tall conifers in large gardens as breeding sites.

BULLFINCH

Pyrrhula pyrrhula

KEY FACTS

Found: *Gardens, hedgerows*
Length: *Up to 17 cm*
Present: *January to December*
Food: *Seeds and berries*
Often seen: *On a perch*
Similar to: *Chaffinch*
Behaviour: *Shy*
Lives for: *Up to 9 years*
Nests: *Bushes or small trees*
Eggs: *4 to 5 greeny blue eggs
with brown speckles*
Broods: *2 per year*
Sexes: *Female is dusky pink*
In UK: *Throughout*

LOOK/LISTEN FOR

Black cap and face
•
Red belly (male)
•
White rump visible in flight
•
Soft tooting contact call
between males and females
•
Long wings and tail
•
Fast undulating flight

VOICE

A soft regular "toot" sound may be a clue that bullfinches are in the area. This is the sound that pairs make to keep in touch with each other. Less often heard is the song of the male bullfinch, which is made up of an odd series of squeaks and rasping notes as though an alien is communicating from another planet. Bullfinches were kept as caged pets by the Victorians in the belief that they could be trained to mimic the songs of other birds.

THESE SHY BIRDS HIDE THEMSELVES away for most of the year, which is something of an achievement given the bright colour of the male's belly. Pairs nest in dense undergrowth in the spring and summer, then roam the hedgerows in the autumn and winter. Their ability to strip fruit trees of tasty buds makes them unpopular with farmers and gardeners.

FEEDING THE YOUNG

The chicks are fed a mixture of squidgy insects such as caterpillars and snails, as well as softened seeds. Unlike the other finches in this book, the parents carry food back to the nest in special throat pouches. When full, they make the adults' cheeks looked puffed out.

FEMALE

The gentle colours of the female bullfinch make her much harder to spot than the male. The young are similarly pale in colour but don't have her black cap.

IN THE GARDEN

Bullfinches prefer gardens close to woodland or scrub where they can flee if alarmed. Scattering seeds on bird tables may encourage them in, but they are likely to visit only from the autumn to early spring. If you have hawthorn, blackthorn or cherry trees nearby, bullfinches may descend to eat the buds as they appear in spring.

LESSER REDPOLL

Acanthis caberet

LOOK/LISTEN FOR

Red forehead (male)

•

Tiny black bib

•

Trilling flight call

•

Hanging acrobatically from riverside tree branches

•

Streaked appearance

•

Forked tail

VOICE

Male birds have two main reasons for singing: to tell other males "this is my patch, stay away," and to say to females "I'm gorgeous, be my mate." Lesser redpolls are happy to nest in groups and so have no need for the territorial song. When displaying to females, they perform a mix of trills and rattling notes while circling overhead. Their flight call is a very fast "cheep-cheep-cheep" with other notes mixed in.

THE FINCH FAMILY

The lesser redpoll is part of the finch family. Seven of them are featured in this book, but in all, there are over 100 different species. They are generally sociable birds, spending time outside the breeding season in flocks. They have strong beaks for cracking seeds and a bouncy way of flying.

BARELY BIGGER THAN A BLUE TIT, the lesser redpoll is one of our smallest finches. It hangs off tree branches at all angles in its search for tiny seeds to eat, such as alder and birch. If disturbed, flocks fly up into the air in a mass before circling round and coming back down to rest. Like many bird species, lesser redpoll numbers have fallen sharply in recent years probably because of habitat loss.

KEY FACTS

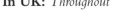

Found: *Gardens, birch woods*
Length: *11.5 cm*
Present: *January to December*
Food: *Seeds*
Often seen: *In trees*
Similar to: *Linnet*
Behaviour: *Nervous*
Lives for: *Up to 6 years*
Nests: *In small trees*
Eggs: *4 to 5 pale blue eggs with brown blotches*
Broods: *2 per year*
Sexes: *Female is less red*
In UK: *Throughout*

FEMALE

Smaller than the male, the female is paler and less streaked and doesn't develop the red breeding colours of the male on his chest and face. Young lesser redpolls lack the red forehead and black bib.

IN THE GARDEN

It is always a joy to see these jaunty birds appear in the garden. They roam in flocks, often with siskins and goldfinches, and may be here one day and gone the next. Hanging feeders present no problems for these acrobatic birds, with February being a likely month for them to visit – especially if you put out niger seeds.

REED BUNTING

Emberiza schoeniclus

KEY FACTS

Found: *Reedbeds, gardens*
Length: *16 cm*
Present: *January to December*
Food: *Seeds and insects*
Often seen: *On the ground*
Similar to: *Dunnock*
Behaviour: *Bold*
Lives for: *Up to 9 years*
Nests: *Mounds in reedbeds*
Eggs: *4 to 5 light brown eggs
with black marbling*
Broods: *2 per year*
Sexes: *Female smaller, browner*
In UK: *Throughout*

LOOK/LISTEN FOR

Black head and bib with
white collar (male in the
breeding season)

•

Streaked back

•

White tail sides

•

Flicking tail

•

Male singing from a perch in
spring and early summer

VOICE

From an open spot at the top of a tall reed or low bush, the male sings his simple song. This is made up of a few repeated notes, ending with a chirruping trill. The speed with which the male sings depends on whether he has found a mate or not. If the first few notes are slow and deliberate, all is well and he has found a female; if the notes are fast, he is still on the look-out for a mate. Listen for the reed bunting's contact call – a squeaky "tsiu" sound – as well.

THIS SINGING MALE is displaying his smart black breeding plumage as he perches on a reed. Sometimes, if danger threatens, reed buntings are known to pretend to have a broken wing to draw the predator away from the nest. The number of reed buntings varies during the year as some fly here to breed in spring, while others arrive in the autumn to escape the cold weather in northern Europe.

NESTING

The female finds a mate in the spring and builds a grassy nest on a mound hidden by reeds. Reed buntings are not very loyal to their mates – males often have several females nesting in the area and females may mate with more than one male. The chicks are fed by both parents and leave the nest after about two weeks.

FEMALE

The wonderfully streaked feathers of the female are similar to the male's colouring in winter and to that of a young reed bunting. She also has a marked light eye stripe.

IN THE GARDEN

It is only during harsh winters, when snow or frost covers grass and other food sources, that reed buntings appear in gardens. Scattering seeds on the ground is the best way to attract them, although some may perch on hanging feeders as well. Look for them flicking their tail feathers as they feed or perch.

PHEASANT

Phasianus colchicus

LOOK/LISTEN FOR

Long, barred tail

•

Red face, small "horns" and coppery underparts (male)

•

Pale beak

•

Whirring flight with short wings

•

Explosive squawk if disturbed

VOICE

In early spring, the male finds an open space to perform his best female-attraction techniques. This involves strutting around and delivering a far-reaching "coo-cuck" followed by vigorous wing-flapping. Pheasants are not famous for their singing ability. They can be heard throughout the year, with all their calls being chicken-like clucks or crows.

TYPES OF PHEASANT

The scientific name *Phasianus colchicus* derives from the place – the River Phasis in the ancient Asian country of Colchis – where the pheasant originated. It was introduced in the 11th century as a game bird, with five more species having been imported since then. The white neck band of the bird in the main picture is that of the most commonly seen Mongolian species.

KEY FACTS

Found: *Gardens, farms, woods*
Length: *71 cm*
Present: *January to December*
Food: *Seeds and insects*
Often seen: *On the ground*
Similar to: *Nothing else*
Behaviour: *Bold*
Lives for: *Up to 7 years*
Nests: *On the ground in undergrowth*
Eggs: *8 to 15 olive-brown eggs*
Broods: *1 per year*
Sexes: *Female is brown*
In UK: *Throughout*

PHEASANTS ARE THE DRAMA QUEENS of the bird world. If disturbed, they squawk explosively and rocket upwards or run away in a state of panic. Males are fiercely territorial, fighting other males with their claws or launching attacks on people, other animals and even cars. By day, groups of females led by a male forage on the ground in open countryside, flying up into trees at night to roost.

IN THE GARDEN

Strutting around the garden with a bevvy of females in tow, the male pheasant looks proud and important. If you live in the countryside, you will be familiar with these large birds and their crowing. Leave out scattered seeds to encourage them to visit regularly, as well as ash remains from fires for them to bathe in.

FEMALE

The mottled brown colouring of the female keeps her hidden in the undergrowth, especially when she is sitting on her nest. Her tail is noticeably shorter than the male's.

SPARROWHAWK
Accipiter nisus

KEY FACTS

Found: *Gardens, woodland, farmland*
Length: *28 to 40 cm*
Present: *January to December*
Food: *Small birds*
Often seen: *Soaring*
Similar to: *Kestrel, goshawk*
Behaviour: *Secretive*
Lives for: *Up to 10 years*
Nests: *Platform in tree branches*
Eggs: *4 to 5 pale blotchy eggs*
Broods: *1 per year*
Sexes: *Female larger, browner*
In UK: *Throughout*

LOOK/LISTEN FOR

Barred breast
•
Yellow legs
•
Short wings, long tail
•
Yellow/orange eyes
•
Flap, flap, glide flight
•
High-pitched "kek-kek-kek" alarm call

VOICE

Sparrowhawks do not produce a wide range of sounds. The two most common ones are a rapid "kek-kek-kek-kek" cry of alarm and a short mewing contact call. Hungry chicks in the nest cry out loudly demanding food from the parents. When the male arrives with a tasty morsel, he announces his presence to the female, sometimes leaving the food on a nearby post.

YOUNG FEMALE

As with many birds of prey, the female is larger than the male and almost twice as heavy. This young sparrowhawk displays the female's browner colour.

THIS RAPTOR IS A LETHAL HUNTER. From hiding in trees it swoops down to make surprise attacks on songbirds, grabbing them in mid-air or from nearby feeders. The female preys on larger birds during the breeding season, pinning them to the ground with her sharp talons and pecking them to death. Sparrowhawks are in turn preyed on by owls, other hawks, foxes and pine martens.

IN THE GARDEN

Sadly, the best way to attract these handsome hawks to your garden is to have a lot of songbirds feeding there. The male sparrowhawk favours tits, finches and sparrows, while the female commonly attacks thrushes and starlings. If you have a large garden with conifers there is a chance they may nest there, too.

COURTSHIP

On bright days in late winter, the male sparrowhawk begins his courtship display by circling high in the air over his territory. Once paired with a female, he builds a twiggy nest, sometimes taking over an old one that once belonged to a squirrel or pigeon. The best way to tell that it is a sparrowhawk nest is to check that all the larger twigs are lined up in the same direction.

STOCK DOVE
Columba oenas

LOOK/LISTEN FOR

Metallic-green neck feathers

•

Pink legs and feet

•

Black wing bars and black wing edges

•

Dark eyes

•

Purple chest feathers

•

"Wooo-wuup" song

VOICE

From February, the male stock dove performs his "wooo-wuup" song to attract a nearby female. He repeats each phrase six times or more, getting louder and faster, before pausing and starting again. To warn other male stock doves to keep away, he repeats a single "coo" from a high branch.

THE PIGEON FAMILY

Doves and pigeons all belong to the same family, with the word dove being used to describe the smaller of the species – like this one. There are around 300 types of pigeon worldwide, the five in the UK being the woodpigeon, collared dove, rock dove, turtle dove and stock dove. Woodpigeons are by far the largest and are easy to spot with their white neck patches and wing bars. Stock doves will join flocks of other pigeons in the autumn and winter, roaming farmland in search of seeds.

KEY FACTS

Found: *Gardens, farms, woods*
Length: *32 to 34 cm*
Present: *January to December*
Food: *Seeds*
Often seen: *On the ground*
Similar to: *Woodpigeon, feral pigeon*
Behaviour: *Timid*
Lives for: *Up to 9 years*
Nests: *In tree holes, nest boxes*
Eggs: *2 creamy white eggs*
Broods: *2 to 3 per year*
Sexes: *Alike*
In UK: *Mostly England, Wales*

SMALLER THAN A WOODPIGEON and easy to confuse with feral pigeons, the stock dove often goes unnoticed. It is the only member of the pigeon and dove family to breed in tree cavities although it does use old buildings and rabbit burrows as well. Tree holes are commonly found in ancient woodland and as these have been cut down in recent years, stock dove numbers are declining.

IN THE GARDEN

These nervous birds will forage under hanging feeders or peck at seeds scattered on bird tables or on the ground. Like all pigeons, they drink a lot of water, so keep a fresh supply available. Stock doves do use nest boxes that are large enough for them to fit into, such as those designed for barn owls.

NECK FEATHERS

You can see the shiny green tips of the stock dove's neck feathers above. Young stock doves, known as squabs, don't get these until after their first moult.

WOODPIGEON
Columba palumbus

KEY FACTS

Found: *Gardens, farmland, woodland, towns*
Length: *40 to 42 cm*
Present: *January to December*
Food: *Crops, clover, fruit, seeds*
Often seen: *In flocks*
Similar to: *Stock dove*
Behaviour: *Sociable*
Lives for: *Up to 10 years*
Nests: *Stick platform in a tree*
Eggs: *2 glossy white eggs*
Broods: *2 to 3 per year*
Sexes: *Alike*
In UK: *Throughout*

LOOK/LISTEN FOR

Soft cooing sound

•

Blue-grey body with white neck patches

•

Flocks in winter

•

Yellow irises

•

Small head and plump body

•

White wing bars when flying

THERE IS SOMETHING rather unfeathery and unreal about the woodpigeon with its smooth blue-grey body, ridged metallic-green neck and beady yellow eyes. It waddles awkwardly on its short legs when on land and makes lots of noise on take-off, but flies gracefully once in the air. Large flocks gather in the autumn and winter, scouring farmland for seeds from weeds and crops.

VOICE

There are few sounds as soothing as the gentle coo of the woodpigeon which can be heard for much of the year. It repeats five deep notes several times – "coo-COO-coo, coo-coo" – unlike the collared dove with its shorter three-note song. Less restful is the loud clapping noise the woodpigeon's wings make as it bursts out of trees. The male also claps its wings in aerial courtship displays as it rises into the air, glides and then dives downwards.

REARING YOUNG

Pigeons have been known to breed in all months. Two eggs are laid at a time and the young chicks are fed on a milky substance produced in the pigeon's crop – a special pouch in its throat. The only other birds that can produce this milky substance are penguins and flamingos.

SQUAB

This baby pigeon, or squab, could win a "chick least-like-its-parent" competition with its long beak and scruffy feathers. At the age of six months, it moults and the white neck markings appear.

IN THE GARDEN

More woodpigeons than ever are appearing in towns as well as the countryside. You may see them perching uncomfortably on the top of hanging feeders, wondering how to reach the seed, or pecking around on the ground at spillages – all types of seed are popular. Some are so tame they can even be fed by hand.

COLLARED DOVE
Streptopelia decaocto

LOOK/LISTEN FOR

Black neck collar

•

Triple cooing song

•

Small flocks in the autumn and winter

•

Red eyes

•

Red legs

•

Pale tail band visible in flight

VOICE

In the spring, the male collared dove joins in the dawn chorus about 20 minutes before the sun rises. His gentle "cu-cooo-cuk" stands out from the trills and warbles of songbirds. To make this cooing sound, he uses his puffed-up throat instead of opening his beak like most birds. The flight call of the collared dove is not restful like its song and is more like the sound of someone playing a kazoo – badly.

NESTING

Like the woodpigeon, the male collared dove performs an impressive courtship flight display. Once paired, the male and female build a twiggy nest hidden away in trees, where they rear two chicks. The male sits on the eggs during the day and the female incubates them at night. Once hatched, the chicks are ready to leave the nest after three weeks.

THE GERMAN NAME for this bird is *die Fernsehtaube* which means "television dove" due to its habit of sitting on TV aerials. Originally from India, collared doves have spread rapidly through Europe since the 1930s and they are now common wherever there are houses and farmyards with trees nearby for nesting. Having up to six broods a year has helped this bird's meteoric spread.

IN THE GARDEN

Many towns and villages are alive with the cooing of collared doves as they prefer to live near humans, especially where there are supplies of seeds nearby. Putting out any form of seed on the ground will attract them, as will water. Unlike many birds who drink by tipping their heads back, pigeons can suck water up.

KEY FACTS

Found: *Gardens, farms, towns*
Length: *31 to 33 cm*
Present: *January to December*
Food: *Grain, seeds, fruit*
Often seen: *On a perch*
Similar to: *Turtle dove*
Behaviour: *Sociable*
Lives for: *Up to 18 years*
Nests: *Stick platform in a tree*
Eggs: *2 glossy white eggs*
Broods: *Usually 2 to 3 per year but can have up to 5*
Sexes: *Alike*
In UK: *Throughout*

TURTLE DOVE

This close relation is fast declining and near to extinction in the UK. It is a summer visitor with a purring coo, patterned wings and orange eyes (see page 57).

TAWNY OWL

Strix aluco

KEY FACTS

Found: *Gardens, woodland*
Length: *Up to 46 cm*
Present: *January to December*
Food: *Mammals, birds, frogs*
Often seen: *Roosting*
Similar to: *Nothing else*
Behaviour: *Nocturnal*
Lives for: *Up to 10 years*
Nests: *Holes in trees, nest boxes*
Eggs: *2 to 4 white eggs*
Broods: *1 per year*
Sexes: *Female is bigger*
In UK: *England, Wales and Scotland*

LOOK/LISTEN FOR

Night-time hooting

•

Disc-like face

•

Dark eyes

•

Owls roosting close to tree trunks during the day

•

Short tail

•

Streaked underside

THIS IS OUR MOST COMMON OWL and it is easier to hear than it is to see, for its brown mottled feathers hide it among the branches of the trees in which it roosts. Finding pellets around tree trunks may mean you have a tawny owl nearby: the pellets are the regurgitated remains of bones and other indigestible food it has eaten. These owls form pairs when they are a year old and stay together for life.

VOICE

The song of the male often starts with a clear "hoo" followed by a more wobbly "hoo-hoo". This is frequently heard a few hours after dusk and in the early hours of the morning. Tawny owls are vocal in the breeding season from March to May and even more so when the young owls are establishing their territories in the autumn. Listen for their loud "ke-wick" contact call as well.

HUNTING

The tawny owl hunts in the dead of night using its sharp sense of hearing to locate its prey. Not only can it hear ten times better than a human, its ears sit at different heights, helping it to pinpoint sounds more easily. Patiently, the owl waits for an animal to move in the undergrowth, then swoops down silently to grasp it in its talons

CHICK

Many tawny-owl chicks fall to the ground as they practise moving along branches near their nest. Parents locate them by their screechy begging contact calls.

IN THE GARDEN

Tawny owls are woodland creatures but many also make their homes in large gardens and parks with old trees. They hoot to mark their territory and once settled rarely venture far away. Tawny owls will occupy nest boxes especially if there is a shortage of tree holes around in which to raise their young.

SWIFT

Apus apus

LOOK/LISTEN FOR

Long wings making an
anchor shape in the sky

•

Small head and pale throat

•

Screaming flocks flying
over villages in summer

•

Shallow forked tail

•

Cup-shaped nests
under eaves

VOICE

The screaming cry of the swift seems
to be loudest at dawn and dusk and
is given as birds race through the
air at lightning speed. The scream
is actually a high-pitched trill, with
the male's cry being lower than
that of the female. Most of their
calls, including the begging cries of
the chicks, are based around these
high-pitched notes.

FLIGHT

Its ability to travel at speeds of up
to 69 miles an hour makes this one
of the world's fastest birds. Almost
everything it does except rearing
chicks is done mid-air including
sleeping, feeding and mating and
once the young leave the nest,
they won't land for at least two
years. In fact, its toes are so small,
walking is almost impossible and
they are useful only for clinging
onto surfaces.

KEY FACTS

Found: *Gardens, town, lakes*
Length: *17 cm*
Present: *May to September*
Food: *Insects*
Often seen: *Flying*
Similar to: *Swallow*
Behaviour: *Sociable*
Lives for: *Up to 17 years*
Nests: *Holes in roofs
and nest boxes*
Eggs: *2 to 3 white oval eggs*
Broods: *1 per year*
Sexes: *Alike*
In UK: *Throughout*

FROM MAY TO SEPTEMBER, the skies above towns and
villages may be filled with the screaming of swifts
travelling in flocks. They feed on a wide variety of flying
insects and drink by flying low over water. A nesting adult
travels miles in search of food for its chicks, collecting
large numbers of insects at a time which it stores as a
food ball in a pouch just below its beak.

IN THE GARDEN

Swifts nest in crannies under the roofs of buildings, in cliffs and
sometimes in tree holes. The nests are composed of grass and
feathers bound together with the bird's saliva. Swifts are known
to use nest boxes such as "swift bricks" which have hollowed-out
centres where the birds can raise their young.

BARN SWALLOW

Another summer migrant, the
barn swallow is similar to the swift
but its undersides are white, its tail
is more heavily forked and it tends
to fly lower in the sky.

GREEN WOODPECKER
Picus viridis

LOOK/LISTEN FOR

Bouncy flight
•
Red cap and pale eyes
•
Vivid green upperparts
and yellow rump
•
Pecking at anthills
•
Laughing call
•
Large, sharp beak

KEY FACTS

Found: *Gardens, farms, parks*
Length: *32 cm*
Present: *January to December*
Food: *Insects, mainly ants*
Often seen: *On the ground*
Similar to: *Nothing else*
Behaviour: *Timid*
Lives for: *Up to 15 years*
Nests: *In a hole in a tree*
Eggs: *5 to 7 white eggs*
Broods: *1 per year*
Sexes: *Female has black face markings, not red*
In UK: *Not in Ireland*

"HA-HA-HA-HA-HA-HA-HA-HA-HA-HA-HA-HA" goes the green woodpecker. No other garden bird makes this laughing sound, and finding one hunting for ants on the grass is a magnificent sight. It is quick to fly away if disturbed, so keeping very still is the best way to watch it. Once rumbled, it flies off with a bouncy flap, flap, flap, glide through the air and a flash of its yellow rump.

VOICE

Woodpeckers are famous for the way they drum on trees with their beaks to mark their territory. Green woodpeckers do drum but far less frequently than great spotted woodpeckers and with a much quieter drilling sound. Their calls are shorter versions of the laughing songs that are used in the spring in courtship displays. It is the song that led to this woodpecker's "yaffle" nickname.

ANATOMY

Its four strong claws and stiff, short tail help this woodpecker to grip on to tree trunks. Yet it spends most of its time on the ground, using its long sticky tongue to lap up as many ants as possible. When it is not being used, the tongue coils away into the back of its head. Males have red "moustaches" like the bird shown here and females have black ones.

JUVENILE

The young look like the adults, but their feathers are streaked and spotted. The red crowns and face markings begin to appear in the autumn of their first year.

IN THE GARDEN

Many large gardens are home to green woodpeckers. They rely on mature or rotten trees where they can make their nest holes and open grassy areas where they can feed. Green-woodpecker numbers are at risk when it is freezing outside and not even their large sharp beaks can pierce the ground to reach any ants.

LOOK/LISTEN FOR

Large white shoulder stripes
and spotted wings

•

Drumming sound

•

Red undertail

•

"Kik-kik" alarm call

•

Large pointed beak

•

Red nape (male)

GREAT SPOTTED WOODPECKER
Dendrocopos major

KEY FACTS

Found: *Gardens, woodland*
Length: *23 cm*
Present: *January to December*
Food: *Insect grubs, nuts, seeds*
Often seen: *Gripping trunks*
Similar to: *Lesser spotted
woodpecker*
Behaviour: *Nervous*
Lives for: *Up to 11 years*
Nests: *In a hole in a tree*
Eggs: *4 to 7 glossy white eggs*
Broods: *1 per year*
Sexes: *Female lacks red nape*
In UK: *Rarely in Ireland*

VOICE

This nervous bird has a distinctive "kik-kik" alarm call but it is probably best known for the drumming sound it makes with its beak against tree trunks, hollow branches and even lamp posts, especially in the spring to mark its territory. The chicks make demanding squeaky noises from the nest as they wait hungrily for their parents to bring food back to them.

NESTING

From late winter, male and female great spotted woodpeckers chase each other noisily through the woods and, once paired, make their nest holes in tree trunks. Here, the female lays four to seven white eggs in May and both parents take turns to sit on them until they hatch. Eggs laid in holes are often white because they are already hidden and have no need to be camouflaged.

THE GREAT SPOTTED WOODPECKER is about the size of a thrush, although its striking colouring and the name "great" makes it seem bigger than this. It feeds on juicy grubs as well as on nuts and seeds which it lodges into crevices and strikes with its sharp beak. There is a special layer of tissue between the base of its bill and its skull to absorb the shock of the vibrations as it drums.

IN THE GARDEN

More gardens than ever before have great spotted woodpeckers taking peanuts and suet balls from hanging feeders. They grip on to the wire containers like oversized blue tits, nervously scouring the area for danger. At the slightest noise, they fly off to the safety of a nearby tree before returning to resume feeding.

JUVENILE

This fledgling's crown will turn black after its first moult. The adult female's head is black and white while the male has a red patch at the back of his neck.

JACKDAW
Corvus monedula

KEY FACTS

Found: *Gardens, farms, towns*
Length: *34 cm*
Present: *January to December*
Food: *Almost anything*
Often seen: *On the ground*
Similar to: *Carrion crow, rook*
Behaviour: *Bold*
Lives for: *Up to 17 years*
Nests: *In holes in trees, chimneys and ruins*
Eggs: *4 to 5 pale speckled eggs*
Broods: *1 per year*
Sexes: *Alike*
In UK: *Throughout*

LOOK/LISTEN FOR

Light grey neck collar

•

Dark cap and face

•

Pale eyes

•

"Chack" call

•

Strutting around in pairs

•

Large flocks feeding and roosting together

IF YOU SEE ONE JACKDAW strutting around, look for another one nearby. These birds mate for life and are rarely seen on their own. They are smaller than other members of the crow family and have thinner beaks, rounder heads and remarkable pale eyes which often look a piercing blue colour. Strangely, they may well be seen riding on the backs of sheep and horses, looking for parasites to eat.

VOICE

These are noisy birds and their loud "chack" call can be heard all year round. Flocks chatter as they fly as well as when they perch, particularly when they are settling down at night to roost. They have a range of calls which vary in tone and length and are used in different situations.

THE CROW FAMILY

This is a large family of birds, which includes jackdaws, magpies, jays, rooks, ravens and carrion crows; the latter is the one most frequently referred to just as a crow. They are all highly intelligent birds which scavenge for food and make a range of croaking calls. Outside the breeding season you may see many of these species gathering in large flocks. The collective noun for crows is a murder or a mob and for ravens it is an unkindness.

NESTING

In the spring, jackdaws carry large amounts of nesting material in their beaks. Their nests are lined with soft materials such as wool plucked from the backs of sheep.

IN THE GARDEN

A great frequenter of the church/ Where, bishop-like, he finds a perch/ And dormitory, too. "The Jackdaw" by William Cowper (1731–1800)
These inquisitive birds often nest in the roofs of churches and houses and in chimney pots. They visit gardens hoping to find scraps of food; if you feed them, it may frighten off songbirds.

MAGPIE

Pica pica

LOOK/LISTEN FOR

Long glossy tail

•

White shoulder and belly

•

Dark beak, legs and eyes

•

Gangs of birds in late winter

•

Loud rattling call

•

Domed twiggy nest in the fork of a tall tree

VOICE

Magpies are not musical birds. Their calls range from a single harsh "chack" to rattling volleys of similar-sounding notes – "chack-ack-ack-ack" – with short pauses in between. Their song is much softer and is composed of musical trills, whistles and barking sounds but it is given only around the nesting site and is rarely heard.

NESTING

Unlike the other members of the crow family featured here, the magpie builds an impressive nest. First, it creates a bowl out of sticks and lines it with earth, with an inner layer of small roots and grasses. Then it makes a protective dome out of thorny twigs, forming an ideal place in which to keep its chicks safe and warm. The nest may be finished two months before egg-laying starts in April.

KEY FACTS

Found: *Gardens, farms, towns*
Length: *45 cm*
Present: *January to December*
Food: *Almost anything*
Often seen: *On the ground*
Similar to: *Nothing else*
Behaviour: *Bold*
Lives for: *Up to 21 years*
Nests: *In larger trees*
Eggs: *4 to 6 greeny blue eggs with brown speckles*
Broods: *1 per year*
Sexes: *Female has shorter tail*
In UK: *Throughout*

MAGPIES ARE STRIKING-LOOKING birds with black-and-white plumage and iridescent feathers. It is hard to tell the difference between the sexes but females are less glossy and have shorter tails. Look for magpies in early spring gathered in groups in trees, chattering and chasing one another. Scientists have found that magpies are one of the few animals that can recognise themselves in mirrors.

IN THE GARDEN

These aggressive birds are rarely welcome in gardens because of their raucous calling and habit of raiding songbird nests as they search for eggs and chicks to feed to their young. You can hear smaller birds calling out in alarm as a magpie approaches. If you want to deter them, try hanging shiny objects in trees.

FLIGHT

The magpie flies with strong steady wing beats. In the picture above, you can see the white border to its wings as it carries a twig back to its nest.

JAY

Garrulus glandarius

FAMILY: CROWS

KEY FACTS

Found: *Gardens, woodland*
Length: *34 cm*
Present: *January to December*
Food: *Almost anything*
Often seen: *In trees*
Similar to: *Nothing else*
Behaviour: *Shy*
Lives for: *Up to 16 years*
Nests: *In larger trees*
Eggs: *4 to 6 freckled green eggs*
Broods: *1 per year*
Sexes: *Alike*
In UK: *Throughout except north Scotland*

THIS COLOURFUL BIRD is very nervous and for most of the year it moves around alone or in small groups, unlike some other crows which tend to be more sociable. In their cup-shaped nest made of twigs, the parents raise one brood in the spring. Both the male and the female jay feed the young, chasing them out of their territory once they are seven weeks old.

FLIGHT FEATHERS

A flash of its bright blue feathers and its white rump may be all you see of the secretive jay as it darts between trees.

IN THE GARDEN

The jay is largely a woodland bird, but it does visit large gardens with trees where it can hide. It is increasingly seen at feeding stations, where it may try to cling on to hanging feeders. However, it is happiest if there is food scattered on the ground or on a table – mealworm and peanuts are popular, but it is not a fussy eater.

LOOK/LISTEN FOR

Harsh screeching call

•

Darting between trees

•

White rump

•

Blue striped wing feathers

•

Pale eyes and black cheek markings

•

Hiding acorns in the autumn

VOICE

You are more likely to hear than to see this noisy creature as its screaming cries pierce the air. A screech may be made once, twice or several times, and is used in alarm or to advertise its presence to other birds. Like all members of the crow family, the jay is extremely intelligent and can imitate the sounds of other birds calling out to their young. If found, the hapless chicks may become the jay's next meal.

HOARDING ACORNS

Jays rely heavily on acorns to get them through the winter. They collect them in the autumn and hide them in holes in the ground or tree cavities, returning to unearth them when other food sources have dried up. A single bird may hide several thousand in its outdoor larder annually; ones it forgets may form new oak trees.

CARRION CROW
Corvus corone

LOOK/LISTEN FOR

Harsh "craa-craa-craa" call

•

Light-catching plumage with a greeny purple sheen

•

Stout beak with feathers at the base

•

Mixed in with rooks and jackdaws in autumn flocks

•

Rounded head

VOICE

"Craa" goes the carrion crow, usually three to six times in a row. It is an unmusical rasping sound delivered with neck outstretched and body moving from side to side. If a threat such as a cat ventures near, the crow's cries become even more intense. The rook makes a slightly longer "kraaa" sound – try standing next to a rookery to get the full effect.

NESTING

In early February, carrion crows start their breeding displays. The male spreads his wings and tail feathers and bows to impress his female partner. A pair will stay together for life, raising one brood each year in their twiggy nest in the fork of a tree. When the chicks fledge, they stay with their parents for several weeks or more, after which some leave to form bands with other young crows.

KEY FACTS

Found: *Gardens, farms, towns*
Length: *47 cm*
Present: *January to December*
Food: *Almost anything*
Often seen: *On the ground*
Similar to: *Rook, jackdaw*
Behaviour: *Bold*
Lives for: *Up to 17 years*
Nests: *In the forks of trees*
Eggs: *3 to 6 blue spotted eggs*
Broods: *1 per year*
Sexes: *Alike*
In UK: *Hooded crow replaces it in Ireland and Scotland*

CARRION IS THE TERM for dead animals which form part of this crow's diet. With its gruesome name, jet-black appearance and fierce expression, this common bird has a sinister air. It is much smaller than the equally black raven, but easy to confuse with the similar-sized rook. Rooks, however, nest in noisy colonies and have pale bills, whereas these crows are solitary nesters with dark bills.

IN THE GARDEN

Like most members of the crow family, this is not a popular garden bird and some people take measures to keep it away rather than to attract it. However, it is unusually intelligent and it is definitely worth spending some time watching its behaviour – particularly how it feeds and the way it reacts to other crows.

HOODED CROW

Instead of carrion crows, Scotland and Ireland have hooded crows. These birds are closely related and there is an area where the two species do overlap and interbreed.

RARER VISITORS

For many, birds are the strongest bond to the living world of nature.
Alexander F Skutch, botanist and ornithologist (1904–2004)

THE WONDER OF FEEDING BIRDS in the garden is that no two days are the same. A species may appear suddenly and as quickly it may be gone. Rarer birds may be on migration seeking to refuel, or severe weather might have driven them in when no other food is available.

BLACK REDSTART
Phoenicurus ochruros

There are two types of redstart in the UK – one known simply as a common redstart, with a bright orange breast, and then there is the black redstart, which is greyer. Look for it constantly flicking its rusty tail as it perches on a stone or roof. The male is shown above; females and juveniles are greyer.

Black redstarts are one of the first to sing in the dawn chorus, usually from a high spot such as the top of a building. Some birds spend only the winter here, but a few pairs also stay to breed.

CHIFFCHAFF
Phylloscopus collybita

This has to be the easiest bird song to recognise, for the chiffchaff sings its name. It is a small, energetic member of the warbler family, which migrates to the UK in March. The male finds a perch and moves his head and tail as he delivers his chiff-chaff song. This reaches a peak in spring and early summer as the male looks for a mate.

This bird usually visits gardens only when on migration. If you think you see one, it may be a willow warbler with which the chiffchaff (when silent) is easily confused.

GARDEN WARBLER
Sylvia borin

It is obvious from the images above that the garden warbler and the chiffchaff are from the same family. Despite its name, the garden warbler is not commonly seen in gardens except perhaps on migration in the autumn and spring, as it prefers woodland and thickets with lots of cover.

The most notable thing about this small, olive bird is its beautiful song. On arrival in April, the male sings from early morning onwards to attract a mate. The song is like the blackcap's (see page 20) but has longer phrases.

LESSER SPOTTED WOODPECKER
Dryobates minor

If you live in either England or Wales and have a large garden with mature trees in it, then you may be lucky enough to see the lesser spotted woodpecker.

You can tell that the bird above is a male, for the female lacks the red crown. Both sexes have the striking black-and-white pattern, which you can see on their upper feathers, and a bounding flight style. They are the smallest of the European woodpeckers and roughly the size of a robin.

ROOK
Corvus frugilegus

These large black birds breed in colonies called rookeries. From the beginning of March, rooks go about making their twiggy nests in the tops of tall trees, usually near houses. If you have a rookery near you, you will certainly know about it, for the noise made by the birds during the breeding season can be very loud, especially once the young rooks start begging for food.

During the autumn and winter, rooks roam the countryside in flocks and roost together at night.

TREE SPARROW
Passer montanus

Unlike house sparrows, male and female tree sparrows look alike. Their chestnut caps and black cheek spots make them easy to identify, although you would be lucky to see them outside central and eastern England and the east coast of Ireland.

They used to be widespread in the 1960s but numbers have fallen by 93% since then and they are now on the Red (danger) List for bird conservation. They sometimes take seed from bird tables in the winter and may use nest boxes for breeding.

TURTLE DOVE
Streptopelia turtur

This pretty summer visitor arrives from its African wintering grounds between April and May. It is our only migratory dove and male and female birds look similar. Like the tree sparrow, it is on the Red List for birds. This is one of the species shot in the Mediterranean while on migration. The use of herbicides in farming has also reduced the weeds on which it feeds.

Its sleepy purring call is heard only in the south and east of England between April and late September.

YELLOWHAMMER
Emberiza citrinella

Hedgerows filled with these sunny-coloured birds are a wonderful sight. The yellower male finds an open perch in spring and sings his cheery song, which is said to sound like "a little bit of bread and no chee-ee-se". He keeps his recital going energetically all through the day and is one of the last birds to stop singing in the summer.

Yellowhammers are a type of bunting – a family of birds with flattish heads, long tails, conical beaks and loud songs. They may visit bird tables in the winter if seed is available.

GARDEN BIRDS AND YOU

THE NUMBER OF BIRDS is falling worldwide as a result of habitat loss, climate change and the use of pesticides. Even some of our most common garden birds are in serious decline. By watching and learning about the ones in your garden and by providing them with food, water and shelter, you are playing a vital role in bird conservation. These are a few other ways in which you can help:

•

Join a bird organisation such as the British Trust for Ornithology (BTO); the Royal Society for the Protection of Birds (RSPB); or the Wildfowl and Wetlands Trust (WWT). There may also be a local society monitoring birds close to you.

•

Take part in the RSPB Big Garden Birdwatch – by transmitting data about the birds in your patch you are helping conservationists who work to protect birds.

•

Keep plastic out of your garden, recycle waste and pick up litter you see around you to prevent birds and other animals from ingesting it.

•

If you find injured or sick birds, leave them and let the Royal Society for the Prevention of Cruelty to Animals (RSPCA) know.

•

Buy organic foods to help discourage farmers from using pesticides which kill many of the plants and animals on which birds feed.

> *Great things are done*
> *by a series of small things*
> *brought together.*
>
> Vincent van Gogh,
> painter (1853–1890)

INDEX OF BIRDS

ACKNOWLEDGEMENTS

WITH THANKS TO
Sunita Gahir – Prepress designer
Yolanta Motylinska – Production adviser
Louise Thomas – Picture research
Penny Phillips – Proof reader

What's That Garden Bird? - Picture Credits

KEY: **a** = above, **b** = below, **c** = centre, **l** = left, **r** = right

4al/35c/61 (chaffinch) Vishnevskiy Vasily/Shutterstock; 4ar (bullfinches) photomaster/Shutterstock; 5al (pheasant) Borislav Borisov/Shutterstock; 5ar/7r/11ac/49c (swift) Gallinago Media/Shutterstock; 5cl/7r/17c (house martin) Nick Vorobey/Shutterstock; 5clb (waxwing) Risto Puranen/Shutterstock; 5c (chaffinch) Mark Medcalf/Shutterstock; 5c (great spotted woodpecker) Massimiliano Paolino/Shutterstock; 5c (starling) Sokolov Alexey/Shutterstock; 5cra (great tit) Jozef Sowa/Shutterstock; 5crb/54bl (jay) Wildlife World/Shutterstock; 5bl (pigeon) Allexxandar/ Shutterstock; 5bc (goldfinch) Targn Pleiades/Shutterstock; 6br/24bl (brambling flock) Franke de Jong/Shutterstock; 6ar/7l/29c (redwing) Razvan Zinica/Shutterstock; 6bl/7r/28c (fieldfare) Karin Jaehne/Shutterstock; 6bl/7r/36c (brambling) Mriya Wildlife/ Shutterstock; 6bl/23c (waxwing) Rowland Cole/Shutterstock; 6c (contact calls) Erni/Shutterstock; 6bcr (chiffchaff) Robert Horne; 6al/31c (spotted flycatcher) clarst5/Shutterstock; 6al/49br (barn swallow) Gallinago Media/Shutterstock; 6al/56cr (garden warbler) Nick Vorobey/Shutterstock; 8ar (nest boxes) Ian Sherriffs/Shutterstock; 8ac/36bl (bramblings) Drakuliren/Shutterstock; 10c (greenfinches) Antonio Petrone/Shutterstock; 11bc/20c (blackcap) Victor Tyakht/ Shutterstock; 14bl (coal tit nest) Arco Images GmbH/Alamy; 15c (marsh tit) Bildagentur Zoonar GmbH/Shutterstock; 15br (willow tit) Piotr Krzeslak/Shutterstock; 19br (firecrest) Kasperczak Bohdan/Shutterstock; 22bl (nuthatch) Ihor Hvozdetskyi/Shutterstock; 26bl (song thrush fledgling) Chamille White/Shutterstock; 27c/58ac (mistle thrush) Karel Bartik/Shutterstock; 27br (mistle thrush nest) YK/Shutterstock; 28bl (fieldfare) Martin Pelanek/Shutterstock; 29br (redwing colouring) Erni/Shutterstock; 33br (cuckoo) Piotr Krzeslak/Shutterstock; 34c (pied wagtail) Marcin Perkowski/ Shutterstock; 34bl (grey wagtail) PhotoCatcher/Shutterstock; 37c (greenfinch) John Navajo/Shutterstock; 37br (female greenfinch) Marcin Perkowski/Shutterstock; 38c/7l (goldfinch) Kasperczak Bohdan/Shutterstock; 39br (female siskin) Miroslav Hlavko/Shutterstock; 7r/40c (bullfinch) Olga Lipatova/Shutterstock; 40bl (female bullfinch) ihelgi/Shutterstock 41c (lesser redpoll) Targn Pleiades/Shutterstock; 41cr (female lesser redpoll) Targn Pleiades/Shutterstock; 42c (reed bunting) Erni/Shutterstock; 42bl (female reed bunting) Veselin Gramatikov/Shutterstock; 44c (sparrowhawk) Mark Medcalf/Shutterstock; 44bl (female sparrowhawk) Carl Mckie/Shutterstock; 45c (stock dove) Erni/Shutterstock; 46bl (woodpigeon squab) Eric Isselee/Shutterstock; 47c (collared dove) Szymon Bartosz/Shutterstock; 47br/57cr (turtle dove) Andre Labetaa/Shutterstock; 48bl (tawny owl chick) Mark Caunt/Shutterstock; 50c (green woodpecker) StockPhoto Astur/Shutterstock; 50bl (green woodpecker juvenile) Paul A. Carpenter/Shutterstock; 7l/51c (great spotted woodpecker) Colin Robert Varndell/Shutterstock; 53c (magpie) Juniors Bildarchiv GmbH/Alamy; 54c (jay) Zakharov Aleksey/ Shutterstock; 56l (black redstart) stmilan/Shutterstock; 56cl (chiffchaff) Montipaiton/Shutterstock; 56r (lesser spotted woodpecker) Vitaly Ilyasov/Shutterstock; 57l (rook) xpixel/Shutterstock; 57cl (tree sparrow) Johannes Dag Mayer/ Shutterstock; 7r/57r (yellowhammer) Aleksey Karpenko/Shutterstock.

All other images © Fine Feather Press